# SLOWLY DYING AND LIVING THROUGH IT

## From Addicted Junkie To Self Sufficient Family Man

Ryan Ponn

*I would like to dedicate this book to the memory of Justin Galland*

*I would also like to dedicate this book the Ed Keating Center and all of the men and women that have come through these centers to get the help that they needed. To all of those that have fallen because of this disease, may you rest in peace.*

# PART 1

# CHAPTER 1

◆ ◆ ◆

Do you have a side or opinion for the debate? Do you believe addiction to be a disease? Or do you believe it to be just a choice? Personally, I fall on the "disease" side of this argument. I've used my own experiences and observations to fuel this decision and until I started this book, hadn't realized exactly how many people were on the other side of the fence.

Since this debate had come to light, I've sat down and spoken with several friends and associates about this, forming almost an experimental base in the process. It's been my experience, of course, that addiction is a disease and it seems that there are almost an equal number of people that stand against me on this. I've heard the arguments. "It's just a choice." "Those people chose to put that (insert substance here) into their body." "They're just looking to pass the buck off and not take responsibility for their actions." Many of these people hadn't known about my past when I began asking their opinion. And I am writing this book to submit my argument in favor of addiction being a disease.

First, let's get that last argument out of the way. The first thing that you should know about me is that I am, in fact, an addict. I spent over a decade of my life using and abusing several different substances to the point that there are only a few of them out there that I hadn't tried. And I did this on my own. I am the only one to blame for this. Before you stop reading, believing that

I'm just an addict and you won't be able to take anything away from this book, please understand that I have been sober and free from the clutches of such substances for over six years now. The second thing you should know about this "junkie" is that I take full responsibility for what I've put into my body. They are right about one thing for sure; I chose to use/abuse those substances. Nobody else is to blame here. I took all of the classes in school about anti-drug this and "don't be an alcoholic" that in school. I knew very well what could and would happen. Yet I still did this. But why, many would tend to ask.

It's not that I am arguing that drug addicts didn't have the choice to make, or that they are in some way not responsible for their actions. Quite on the contrary. We addicts made the conscious decision to use and abuse and that is on us. The vast majority of us knew what could/would happen and we continued to use anyway. What I'm proposing is that we were hard-wired to be addicted to something from the beginning. We just wound up using drugs and alcohol to satisfy these urges.

I'm sure that you have heard the term, "Creature of habit." I believe that is a form of addiction. In fact, that's exactly what it is. You see, we are hard-wired to abuse just about anything we enjoy. We can't help but to overindulge, completely ignoring those who preach "everything in moderation." To bolster the point that I'm trying to make, we have already recognized several different addictions in society today. There's the typical addictions such as drug addiction or alcoholism. Then there are the slightly less talked about over-eating and sex addiction. If we enjoy anything to a certain degree, we tend to continue without a way to stop. We become completely enslaved to whatever it is that we simply enjoyed before and throw out all of the warning signs and precautions.

It seems to me that being that we find ourselves to be all

but unable to stop ourselves in these situations, which would be where the disease part comes into play. Yes, we've made our choices, which have led to our own personal Hells, but the root of the problem seems to be found in our patterns prior to consumption or indulgence of whatever our respective choice poison is.

I began to write this book to show readers my life. By doing that, I had hoped to reach two different groups of readers; those that don't know enough about addiction and those who are personally or know someone that is currently addicted. Those that really don't understand addiction, I hope to give them a new view on the issue. Show some of the things that an addict goes through, such as how they think and the ways their lives can slowly slide out of control. For the current addicts, I hope to give them some kind of hope as well. To show them that they can get free from addiction's clutches. I want them to know that there are resources out there that can and will help. Because after all, together we can be sober.

I hope that you, the reader, get what you need from this book, regardless of what that may be. Good luck with all that you do in your life, and may you never (or no longer) have to deal with this disease. As a great friend (one that I will mention later in this book) used to say on a regular basis, "If nobody has told you that they love you today, I love you."

# CHAPTER 2

◆ ◆ ◆

Once an addict, always an addict. That's what they say at least. Hell, maybe it's true even. But I'm not completely buying it. You can't tell me that I will never be better. You cannot seriously tell me that if I used/abused something, even for a significant length of time such as ten years or more, that I will never lead a clean and sober, productive life. That I will never be a decent parent. Or a decent sibling, son, or friend. I know for a fact that I can, because I already have done exactly that.

I should also warn you that I do, and will continue to, refer to addiction as a disease. I know that there are a whole lot of people that disagree with that, but please just hear me out on this one. I have been dealing with this for decades and I am basing my theory off of personal observations. By that I mean things that I have observed about myself and things that I have observed about others. It seems to me that addiction could actually be a disease of the mind. The counter argument is, of course, that the addiction started with a choice. But I maintain that this disease started way before that. I think you should see what I am talking about as you get further into this book. Later on, I will even try to explain my theory in much more detail.

Obviously I wasn't using anything when I was born. In fact, my mother wasn't using anything either. Nor was my father. I grew up with amazing, supportive parents. They were there for me every single step of my life. By all means, I should've become a successful businessman, or a lawyer, or a doctor. I don't know. All I know is that according to almost everybody else's thoughts and opinions, I should've been a successful individual instead of the complete and utter failure that I became.

I'm not saying that I am still a failure, I just was for a good portion of my life. I have found more ways to screw everything up than most people have found to screw up single aspects of their own lives. But I have also found ways to fix just about every one of those things. Luckily, I was able to connect with a group of people that is still there for me when I need them to be.

I was born on New Year's Eve in 1984. I'm not entirely sure of the time so I'm not even going to try to venture a guess. I was born to both Tim and Jane Ponn as their first child, both of which had gone on to prove to the world that they are both outstanding parents. Before me, my father had two other children, but I was my mother's first. My father's first born boy was actually my older brother, who I spent my entire childhood looking up to, and my father's first born child was my sister April, who I had never gotten to meet because of an unfortunate incident where a drunk driver swerved off of the road and hit her. I may have never had the chance to meet her, but I want to go on record as saying that I love her very much. Actually, I've always thought of her as being my angel, looking down on me and keeping me as safe as she can, despite the idiotic shit that I've pulled in my life. My father spent the majority of his time at work during my earlier years of life, while my mother stayed home with me for the vast majority of my childhood with two of my brothers (both younger). At least up until I was in the sixth grade.

At the time of my birth, we were living in Aurora, which is a suburb of Chicago. Actually, it's because of this that I am, and always will be a Chicago sports fan. I will always be a fan of the Bears (who won the Super Bowl immediately after my birth. Just saying). I was staying up late through all of the Bulls' "Repeat Threepeat" era. I was absolutely loving the days after the Cubs beat the Indians in the World Series and despite knowing next to nothing about hockey, I stand behind the Blackhawks no matter what.

I stayed out there up through my Kindergarten years and moved to northeast Ohio during that summer. We lived in a suburb of Cleveland called Mentor. I didn't mind it too terribly much. Of course I didn't want to be there because I have never really been great with change. Especially big changes like that. However, the area was nice enough and I had made a few friends during my time there. My parents tried to make the best of it, that's for sure. After moving there, my father decided that he was going to tear down the dilapidated building that sat behind the house and use the remaining foundation to make a basketball court for us. I spent hours out there practicing because I really believed that I was going to grow up to be something big. Being that I was always pretty tall for my age, basketball just made sense. Spoiler alert: Definitely never became a professional basketball player.

I also tried a few other avenues. I tried working on motors, but quickly found that I would never get past a basic understanding. I got my first drum set while living there, but was definitely not good enough to form a successful band. Trust me. I tried. And let's not forget the period of time that I truly believed that I was going to become a big-time engineer. You see, my father grew up to become a very successful engineer. He worked for several huge corporations, and eventually started his own company while living in our Mentor house. Actually, the company was only half his. The other half belonged to my mother. As for me however, I never did follow through.

# CHAPTER 3

◆ ◆ ◆

In school, I always felt different from everybody else. I felt like I never belonged (which seems to be a common theme among those of us with this disease). I wasn't into sports and I looked up to the bad kids in the neighborhood, although I can't for the life of me remember why. Despite this fact, I still brought home good grades, and if they did drop, it was because I didn't want to do the work. I wasn't being challenged enough and I would start to get complacent. I really didn't get in any trouble while I was that young either, making my inexplicable admiration of the bad kids that much stranger.

For some reason, I was always trying get people to think I was such a bad ass. I don't know why, I just did. For some reason I thought that I could get everybody to think that I was someone that you just didn't mess with. Someone that would beat up anybody that got in his way. However, spoiler alert, I was never that person. I can honestly say that I have never been even close to being that guy. I just used to try to be that guy without anything to back it up.

I also had quite a difficult time trying to make friends. Or at least I thought I did at the time. In all reality, I think I was just seeing it that way. I had a best friend out there and the more I think about it, the more I realize that I also had a few other friends. Honestly, I'm not sure why I had thought that I had any trouble making friends while I lived out there.

This was also about the time that I had started to find music. It wasn't music the way that I listen to now, but music none the less. In the fourth grade I had seen a demonstration from the Elementary School Orchestra Directors/teachers. For some reason, I decided that I wanted to do exactly that. So I went home and spoke to my mom, who went out to a pawn shop and, long story short, I started playing the violin. I wasn't bad either. However, I dropped out of that by the end of the school year. Actually, my mom made me drop out of it. She had given me a choice. Either I could keep going or I could give it up, but if I chose to keep going, I had to put in plenty of practice time. That should have been where I found out that I had a real knack for music. I practiced maybe once a week, but you wouldn't be able to tell just by judging me in the school concerts because I never really missed a cue or a note. Anyway, as a kid I heard "Either you can practice this instrument or you can go play", so I did exactly what most other kids would do and I gave it up.

When my family and I moved out of Mentor, it was February of 1997 and I was in the sixth grade. My parents had found a property out in (seemingly) the middle of nowhere. The small town of Orwell, OH seemed to scream out to them in several ways. The price was affordable and included three fully functional buildings and 93 and a half acres of land, plus two miles of river bank on the Grand River. Being that there were three different functional buildings, it didn't take long before my parents realized that they could move everything from their company, AlpTex Inc., out there and operate the company while staying on their own property. My mom oversaw production and finances in one building and my dad stuck to the other building to head all engineering, machining, and all other new product development. And last but not least, they saw a quaint little town that couldn't possibly be riddled with drugs like the city that we had left. Therefore, wouldn't it be best for their children to be raised out there, in the country, away from the influence of drugs? Theoretically, sure.

Let me point out that if you are trying to keep your kids from experimenting with drugs and alcohol, never, and I mean never, move them out to a small country town. In fact, I can personally guarantee that you will not find a single place in this country that a geographical change will help you keep them (or yourself) drug free. As much as it sounds like a viable way to distance them from that life style and the influences that come with it, you cannot move away from the problem. All you can really do is keep the lines of communication wide open with them and talk them through their problems. Outside of that, nothing else will actually be effective enough.

We all know of the stories about drug problems in the city. Everybody knows that drugs have been running rampant through city streets everywhere. In fact, on more than one occasion it was declared to be an epidemic. But what most people don't seem to realize is that small towns are just as bad, if not worse. Out in small towns, such as the one that we had moved to, most of the youth tend to get bored fast. They're looking for excitement, which can be found by partying. And the wild parties found out there can be absolutely packed with different drugs. I feel like that played a huge part in my problem.

When we first moved out to Orwell, I was actually quite happy. I mean, of course I really missed my friends. However, I still liked it. About a year or two before we moved, I had joined the Boy Scouts of America. Therefore, having so much land at my disposal was exciting to me. When we moved, I had decided to quit the scouts, but I still enjoyed going out and adventuring through the new property. I found several interesting things such as run-down cabins that were all but destroyed from not being taken care of, giant slabs of concrete that the local rattle snakes liked to crawl through (when I found that out, I quit visiting this location), and all of the different spots that the Grand River would leave the random items that it had carried downstream.

This fascination had run its course pretty quickly. It was very soon after we had moved when I simply stopped going out through our property. I wish I could tell you that I knew why, but I don't. My guess would be that I had found a new fascination (some would call an obsession) with video games. Growing up, I really wasn't allowed to have video games. We had my older brother's Atari and that was it for the first decade of my life. Then I got a Game Boy for Christmas, but even then I only got a select few games. So whenever I had a chance to play them at a friend's house, I was all over it, no matter what it was. I'd glue myself to any of them. So when my younger brother and I had found an ad in the Classifieds section of the local paper looking to sell their Super Nintendo, we didn't hesitate. We formed a plan right there to hold a yard sale and sell almost all of our toys so that we could buy this system. However, my mom heard our plan one day and decided to cut us a deal. She would buy it for us, but we had to let our youngest brother play with it too. Obviously we had agreed to it, my mother went and bought the system, and I promptly got lost in this new digital world.

# CHAPTER 4

◆ ◆ ◆

I have always loved different kinds of puzzles. And I have to admit, I tend to obsess over them. In my adult life, I had bought three different versions of the Rubik's cube (a traditional one, a 2X2, and a 1X2X3. That last one was really interesting but really simple). I then spent the vast majority of my free time studying videos and reading online articles and blogs until I figured out exactly how to solve them. I didn't stop until I could do all three from memory, no matter how anybody mixed them up. The problem being that I can't remember how to do it now to save my life. If I enjoy it, I overindulge in it. That is my problem and I will be the first to admit it. At least, I'll be the first to admit it now.

After I finally got my hands on a newer system (this was before Sony ever released their first PlayStation), I couldn't be found outside of the house. To make matters worse, my parents had also given us one of their older computers, which was still new enough to install decent games on. I was absolutely stuck and I definitely didn't care. This was my first taste of feeling like a "normal kid".

Up until this time, I had felt like I wasn't normal. My parents didn't let me do the things that a lot of my classmates did. I wasn't allowed to watch shows like South Park or listen to bands like Korn or Marilyn Manson. While most kids my age were playing games like Mortal Kombat, I wasn't even allowed to watch. These were things that the others got to do. But my parents never let me. I wasn't like any of the others and for some reason, I was ashamed of this. Now that I had my "electronic heaven", I felt like I was like everybody else.

While I finished out my schooling, I would tend to get really good grades. However, those took a big hit when I realized that the other kids saw me as being the smart kid. I remember being invited to the chess club when I got to Orwell and thinking "Why the hell would I want to join that? People will think I'm a loser." I mean, I knew how to play and I was actually pretty good at it. And the ironic part about that situation is that I talk to a lot of the members that were in that club at the time and they are awesome people.

I really didn't party while in school. I would experiment here and there with stuff, but nothing too harsh. As it turns out, nobody really wanted me at their parties. For the most part, I really didn't have any friends throughout high school. I mean, there were others that I got along with, but I seriously think they were being nice ironically and acting like my friends. And it's not that I had no friends at all. I just didn't have very many. Instead, I turned to music.

I think it was my sophomore year that I had finally found music. My mother had just let me finally buy whatever I wanted to when it came to CD's. Her reasoning was because she felt like I listened to it a lot differently than others did. I listened to the music. I paid attention to all of the different instruments and how they intertwined with each other. I was absolutely fascinated. One day, I found myself zoned out on the TV, completely engrossed in an episode of Home Improvements (still one of my most favorite shows). It was one of the later episodes where the kids were all grown up and in high school themselves. While I was watching, the character Mark came down the stairs and strapped to his back, he had a beautifully crafted, jet black guitar. It was a

Fender Strat, or at least it closely resembled one, and it was the most gorgeous instrument that I had ever seen at the time. This was close to Christmas and my parents knew me to never ask for anything, ever. So I felt like that was exactly what I needed to do. So when Christmas came, I wasn't too surprised to see a large box under the tree that looked like it could fit a guitar. However, I was surprised when I opened the box. You see, I had been so excited about the prospect of getting a guitar and looking cool that I had completely forgotten to be specific with what I wanted. So on Christmas morning, when I finally opened that box, I was really surprised to find an acoustic sitting in front of me.

I couldn't figure out what to do with it. I had this completely different image in my head of how this was supposed to "play out", as unrealistic as it was. I thought that I was going to get essentially the same thing as I saw in the show. I was then going to become one of the nest guitarists to ever walk the Earth (despite the fact that I had zero lessons and it turned out that I didn't even know how to hold a guitar correctly). This would happen within a matter of a couple of years. Then everybody would see and/or hear me play and think that I was the coolest person that they had ever met. I would also write these awesome songs (I was into heavy metal at the time. I'm not sure how I had figured that I would even know what an awesome song would necessarily sound like) and become rich beyond my wildest dreams. However, I didn't have a plan for this honky-tonk, back-woods, "needs-to-be-played-in-the-hills-with-a-banjo-and-bare-feet" acoustic guitar.

Let me state right now that I absolutely love the sound of an acoustic guitar these days. When it's played the right way, nothing can compare. It's an amazingly clean and full sound, and I actually still play one. However, that wasn't how I looked at it then. I thought for sure that I had no use for this thing. I played around with it a couple of times the night that I had gotten it, hitting a couple of notes at a time and then putting it down. But I really didn't get serious about it for a little while. I had this feeling like I deserved to live out that delusion that I had of life. It was insane. And I was always trying to find the easy way out. Guitar had to be easy as far as I was concerned. And then I could have all of the riches and fame that I had thought came with it. By the way, that seems to be another common thread amongst us addicts. We are always looking for that quick buck.

About a month had gone by while my new acoustic guitar sat and collected dust. I really didn't have any desire to play this thing. I mean, what would the other kids in school think? Remember, I was in high school and always concerned with trying to be cool or popular, so this became a real problem for me. However, after that month, I had found some way to get grounded. I can't remember exactly what had happened, but I do remember that I was left with nothing to do. I was grounded from the video games. I was grounded from the computer. I was grounded from the phone (remember, this was before cell phones became common place). I wasn't allowed to go anywhere and I wasn't allowed to have anybody over. To me, there just wasn't a point in getting out of bed.

On day number two, I started reviewing the rules because I was bored out of my mind and I desperately wanted to find some kind of loophole. Generally, my parents never left a loophole so I have no idea why I thought that I could find one. But I did notice something. My mom never said anything about the guitar. So I picked up and plucked around on it for a little bit. I have been hooked ever sense.

My senior year in high school was kind of crazy to me. This was when I was probably at my weirdest, and I was proud of that fact. Plus, it seemed like everybody had decided that the cool thing now was to be yourself and embrace that. And there was nobody else doing so like me. I was voted as "Most Wildly Dressed" and "Most Unique" (the latter being something that I take an enormous amount of pride in still to this day). Everybody seemed to decide that they wanted to be my friend, and if anybody tried to pick on me or make fun of me, the others seemed to go after them. I did everything that I could to embrace who I was, which showed. Especially in art class where the teacher would allow me to work on whatever project I wanted to. I would squat down on my chair instead of actually sitting in it and on somedays, I would bring my guitar and amplifier in and just spend the class jamming away. I'm not sure when it all changed for me, but now this side of me seems to emerge periodically.

# CHAPTER 5

◆ ◆ ◆

Throughout high school, I had found a couple of different jobs. My first being for my parents. However, that was kind of short lived because I was lazy. It was a summer job and remember, by this time my parents' company was now on the same property that I lived on. Therefore, all I wanted to do was lay around the house because to me, I had never gone to work. I was just always home.

Every day I would go up to town with my friend and co-worker to the Circle K. The first time I did so, I had gotten a Coca Cola Froster (Circle K's slushy), and I liked it to the point that I went and got one every day after that. In fact, if I didn't have a way to town, I actually worried that I wouldn't get one that day for some reason. Looking back on this I can easily identify what was going on, but at the time I didn't see anything wrong with it.

After that summer, I had gone back to school and shortly thereafter decided it was time for a job elsewhere. After all, I did really enjoy those pay days. I found a small pizza shop that was right down the road from my school. On days that I was scheduled to work, I could just walk there. This worked out for about two months, maybe. After that, I got fired. To this day I have no idea why I had gotten fired exactly. Actually, I am yet to be actually told that I was fired. The manager just stopped putting me on the schedule and after about a month of that, I just quit calling. I felt like I had better things to do than chase what was obviously a dead end. Plus, now I was no longer getting a check. I needed to find something to make money.

Around the time that I had finally given up, one of my friends and fellow musicians offered to take me with him to Middlefield, which is a town that is approximately a half an hour drive away from my home in Orwell. There, I had learned that KFC was hiring. I applied, was called in for an interview, and subsequently hired as a cook/dishwasher. Which is exactly where I stayed for the next two and a half years. This is also where my ability to learn way too much, way too quickly kicked in.

This ability is actually both a blessing and a curse. It's a blessing because no matter where I worked, I was able to branch out really quickly, which meant I was more valuable and I got more hours wherever I worked at. For example, while I was working as a cook at KFC, I was also trained as a dishwasher (actually I think that was the other way around). Within my first three to six months, I insisted on wanting to learn how to run the drive-thru. Very soon after that, I had an itch to learn the dining room counter. No matter where I ever worked, I did exactly this. However, that usually meant that they expected way too much from me at each one of these places, which led to having absolutely no life.

At KFC, I had actually made quite a few friends and it was one of my first experiences making friends with anybody outside of my school system. And I mean that good breed of friends. The ones that always have your back or a shoulder to lean on when you need it. They were fantastic. To this day I know that if I was to reach out to either of the "Onya twins" (That's what I call my friends Tonya and Sonya Tribble and yes, they are actually twins), they would be there for me. There were more than just those two, however, they were the only two that I was able to get ahold of to get permission to use their names in this book.

To me, life wasn't too bad at this point in time. I worked part time at KFC after school and every Wednesday, I went over to Tonya's house where we hung out, played pool, and watched movies with some more of our friends. I didn't have any real responsibilities as of yet and I had already started to pick up music by this time so I would spend a huge portion of my time in the basement of my parents' house, which I had converted into a makeshift studio. Sure, I didn't have a whole lot of friends until the last year of this part of my life, but oh well. I also didn't mind because I did have some great friends right there.

Towards the end of my time with KFC, I had started to grow complacent with my job. I wasn't making as much as I would need to survive once a graduated, so around when I had graduated from high school, I had also put my two weeks' notice in. When asked what I was going to do, I would respond with "I'm going to work at Kraftmaid." because there was a manufacturing plant near my house. I hadn't even applied yet, but for some odd reason, I felt like it was inevitable I guess. The store owner had actually tried to talk me out of leaving about a week from my end date telling me that "all you'll find at Kraftmaid is wood dust." Which made me laugh a bit. I replied to him that all I found at KFC was cooking grease so unless he could give me a substantial raise and/or a promotion, my mind was made up.

For some reason, I had decided to wait until after my last day at KFC before I had decided to submit an application. In fact, I had started to worry immediately that I wouldn't be able to find work. I had waited for a few days afterward and called them. Nothing. In fact, it wasn't until about a week later that I had gotten the interview. By then, I had picked up a job at the local convenience store. The mother of one of my best friends' was the store manager at the time and she hired me on the spot. On my first day, I had gotten a call back about an interview on the following day. I accepted it, but I was extremely skeptical that I was going to get the job. Plus, I already had a new job to celebrate. So I decided to go out and party with some of my friends.

Now, you should probably be aware of my definition of party at the time. There is the normal definition which means a group of people celebrating something together in a festive way, or something like that. Then there is my definition, which is a much smaller group of friends getting as messed up as we can. I remember drinking a whole lot and smoking weed. I also remember someone having cocaine. This was the first time that I was ever exposed to this. Luckily, I must not have been ready to go down that path because I passed up on it. However, I do remember seeing the guy that was using it the next morning. He was an absolute wreck on his bed and could barely lift his head. Which kind of made sense to me. After all, what goes up, must come down. He had continuously talked about how he was going skiing the night before. Over and over again he would declare that it was time to hit the slopes. Then he would laugh about it as if he had never heard it before and do another large line. Now, I am kind of a smart ass and I like to joke with people, so I wrote him a message on his plate and left for my interview while chuckling to myself. Later on I had heard that my comment had hit and the guy wasn't exactly happy about it. Not mad, just not happy. He had finally crawled out of bed and found his plate, sitting by itself in the middle of the table with one simple question written across a napkin that I had left. "How does it feel to be at the bottom of the slopes?"

The ironic part about all of that and my decision to not partake was that years later, I would become even worse than that. I would become an absolute monster, hell bent on destroying myself and everyone and everything in my path. Once I got there, very little could stop me and I had no idea how. I was completely powerless to what I was doing and taking. I even tried to just say no. But that never worked and I was back at it in no time. However, I don't want to get too far ahead of myself.

Once I left the trailer that I had just spent all night partying in, I straightened myself up real quick, and headed to the factory for my interview. The way I had seen it, there was no way that they would take me. I was fresh out of high school and had no manufacturing experience. And if by some strange reason I did get the job, I would have to wait for at least a few weeks before I would find out. I was dead wrong. Not only did I get the job, they wanted me to go for my physical immediately. Like as in after the interview. I was more than happy to do so until I found out that I was also going to have to take a drug test. I had never taken one before so this was very new to me. And I was sweating bullets because, remember, I had smoked the night before. I couldn't believe my luck. How could I have been so stupid as to screw up this perfectly good opportunity before I even started? And better yet, what in the hell was I going to say to my parents when they found out I hadn't gotten the job? It hadn't occurred to me yet that I could've just said that I didn't get it. For some reason I was convinced that they would know immediately why I hadn't gotten the job. On the outside, I made sure that I remained calm, although I still couldn't completely wipe the look of depression, regret, and guilt off of my face. But on the inside, I was absolutely destroying myself. How could you be so stupid Ryan? You've screwed up yet again. It was in the middle of this that the nurse had decided to approach me about the results. In fact, I had almost missed it when she told me. I had passed.

Let me back up to point something out. That mental abuse that I had put myself through, well I am not the only one to do that by far. I mean, I know that most people would have been doing the same thing in this situation, but I've also noticed that this is yet another common thread that we addicts seem to share. On the outside, you may never notice. We may seem downright confident in ourselves. However, on the inside, we always doubt ourselves. And the worst part, that doesn't stop when and addict gets clean and sober. Not at all. Actually, I believe that this is one of the many reasons that it is so difficult for us to get clean and sober and stay that way. We will always beat up on ourselves and tear ourselves down. It's what we do. And when we do get clean, we do so even more when something goes wrong. We instantly take the blame for anything and everything and we are convinced that everybody else is doing the same thing and blaming us. We're convinced that everybody sees us as lesser people. As screw-ups that will never be good enough. And no matter what you say to us to contradict this, we will continue to do so. Chances are, that's just how it is and there's nothing that anybody can do about it. However, the closest we will come to getting rid of this problem is professional help and I encourage all addicts, especially those that are trying to get/stay clean and sober, to get into therapy. Maybe someday I will do the same.

As for my new position with Kraftmaid, I began orientation the week after the physical. There, it was a week long process. They reviewed everything from policies to products and everything in between. I was extremely happy that I had found this because I had gone from $6.65 per hour to $8.50 per hour, I got an automatic 40 hours per week, I got paid weekly, and after a year and a half of working there, I was able to make up to $12.50 per hour. Plus I was getting full benefits. I couldn't believe everything that I had in front of me. And if I had just put my head down and trudged forward, I would've ended up way different. If I would've just made more of an effort, this story would be a whole lot different. But of course, that was not how any of this went.

Within the first month I had begun to try to screw it up. I was calling off for no reason, I was sneaking out at the end of my shift to make sure that they couldn't even ask me to do overtime, and I was just plain being lazy while I was there. I would constantly act like that company owed me everything just for being there and I kept acting like being there was like being in Hell on Earth. In fact, if I were them, I would've walked me out and terminated my employment years before I had actually left. This behavior and attitude also coincided with my first moment of complete euphoria and where I started having my love affair with drugs.

As I had mentioned earlier, I had been a really good kid for the most part. However, I had my moments. Like when I had wanted to fit in so I decided to try smoking weed. I had a lot of friends that swore by it. They swore that it was perfectly amazing and I would feel great. So I decided that I was going to try. In some way or another, I got ahold of some. Then my brother and I stayed up a lot later than my parents so that we wouldn't have to worry about them coming around the corner. I wasn't impressed so after we got done, I went straight to bed. The next morning, I decided that I was going to try it again. Maybe I just did it wrong. And plus, they say that you never get high your first time (That, by the way, is a load of bull. If that was true, nobody would keep going because everybody would see it as pointless). I had a little bit of time before the bus would show up, so how about I try it before I go. That way I don't have to wait all day to try it again.

So that is exactly what I did. I threw away the can that I had used to do so as well. To me, I had thought of absolutely everything that I possibly could have. There was no way that I could have been caught, right? Here are the things that I had not thought about. First of all, most people could tell you that there is a distinct smell to it. Not only is there a distinct smell, but the stronger it is, the better it is. To the point that same of the real strong stuff can be smelled pretty easily from a short distance before it has even been smoked. Once you smoke it, it gets even stronger. And I had chosen my room to do smoke it. I was next to an open window, but let's really think about this. A smell that

28

strong will still be in the air. Plus I forgot that my mother used to have the nose of a bloodhound.

The second thing I hadn't thought to consider is that my mother had absolutely no qualms with searching my things. Therefore, holding on to the seeds and stems would most likely be a horrible idea. And if that wasn't a bad enough idea, I probably should not have stashed them in the area that I had smoked. I'm sure there are plenty more factors that contributed to me getting caught, I just can't think of them specifically at the moment. Either way, I was busted. And lucky me, I have the clever mother.

I had gone off to school that day in the midst of my mom's questioning. She wanted to know what I was doing up in my room because she had come upstairs to get me and my brother only to find that we were both huddled in my window, on my side of the room, which is somewhere that she never thought she would find my brother. She also wanted to know what that smell was, although I am quite sure she already knew why there was a pungent skunk-like aroma in the air. Once I had gotten to school, I had wished, hoped, and prayed that my mother would just give up and I would get away with it. The first two or three classes of the day were absolute hell for me, however, after that I started to loosen up a bit. The thoughts of my inevitable interrogation and/or punishment started to drift away. There was no way this matter would still be at hand by the time I got home. I had surely made it and got away with it. I thought.

Once I got home, a very different scenario played out than the one that I had thought up during school. My mom was fit to be tied. The very first thing that I had noticed was the sunglasses case that was in her hand. When "Wild Wild West" had come out in theaters, one of the fast food chains were selling replica sunglasses that looked like the ones that Will Smith had worn in the movie. My brother and I had begged my mom for them and eventually she caved. I bring that up because every pair was packaged in a plastic case and that was the very same case that I saw in my mother's hand. Incidentally, it was also the very same case that I had used to stash all of the stems and seeds, so I knew immediately that this was not going to be a very warm welcome home to say the least.

First thing my mom did after I got home was present the case to me, opened up so that I could see what was in it, and ask me and my brother what it was. If I remember correctly, our very first game plan came pretty quickly and naturally. Claim ignorance as to what they were. Obviously this didn't work. However, the way she went about it was by claiming that she had taken them to the police because she was suspicious of what they were. Therefore, she already knew the answer and we quickly realized that we needed to come clean.....about what they were. Our next plan came just as quickly. Deny, deny, deny, and when we had her convinced, deny some more. This worked equally well because how would they get into the case and tucked away next to my bed if they weren't mine. And she also already knew that my brother was also to blame, so she made sure not to let him off of the hook in any way. Just because they were next to my bed, did not mean that he was innocent in any way.

I've only seen my father cry three times in my life and my mother has only seen him cry four. The time that I hadn't seen was when my sister had died (May she rest in peace). The other three times, I had been at least a direct cause. That night, my dad saw what I had been doing, and instead of yelling or punishing or even acknowledging it, he sat down and cried. My father, one of the strongest people that I ever knew, had reacted to my drug experimentation by crying. I had not been ready for this and it destroyed me. Even as I write this today, this is one of the hardest things for me to admit. I suddenly feel the need to tell you that today, my father and I have a great relationship and he has told me several times that he is very proud of who I have become so far and who I still can be.

Needless to say, I was definitely punished. My father may not have punished me, but there was still my mom, who was always there to do anything that my dad couldn't. This was just how they were. One of them always complimented who the other one was and vice versa. I was grounded for quite a while, the exact length of time I can't remember. Actually, I believe this was the grounding that I had mentioned earlier. The one that got me going on guitar because I didn't have anything else to do. A normal person (as in someone who is not an addict) would typically think that this should be the end of it. That should have been enough to get me to stop and I should have thought "Wow. That was a bad idea. Probably shouldn't do that again." But I am an addict, so after my punishment, my thought was "Wow. That was a bad idea. Should probably make sure that I don't get caught again."

# PART 2

# CHAPTER 6

◆ ◆ ◆

As I said earlier, when I was younger, I was always trying to make people think that I was cool and kind of bad ass. After I had gotten sober, I had of course realized that I was not and I should just be myself. After all, that was when I had started making a lot of friends when I was in high school. However, I didn't see that. What I did see was all of the drug dealers and drug runners that were depicted in movies as being cool and tough. I saw the people that were in the news and thought about how much people probably didn't mess with them. And I saw all of the news stories about how much money these people were either caught with or had made by doing this. So I had subconsciously decided that I was going to keep trying to be that person.

Once I had gotten out of high school, I was ready to start trying to make more money than I had been so far. As I had said earlier, I had gotten my first factory job and when I did, all I saw was dollar signs. I was ready to work as much as they wanted me to because they told me about overtime being time and a half. Or at least I thought that I was ready.

In all reality I wasn't ready for any of that. I didn't know what work was. In fact, I really knew nothing about how the world worked. After my first Saturday shift I wanted to just crawl into bed and stay there for about a week. Subconsciously I felt like they wanted way too much from me. I mean really, how were they going to ask me to work at work? It cracks me up to see people act like that now. But at that time, I was right out of high school so I thought they were asking way too much. In all reality, there were plenty of people that would've killed for my job, and the pay was absolutely amazing for the time. Considering that I also had very few bills because I was living at my parents' house, I was sitting in a great spot.

I was blowing money without even thinking about it. Once every two to three weeks I would go to my favorite music stores and buy about a thousand dollars' worth of equipment. If I had made the right moves, I would have easily been able to buy a decent sized house and have it paid off before I left there. I was on top of the world and somehow had myself convinced that I was in a horrible situation.

It was around this time that I started feeling the back pain. I thought that it was just from the work. It was much later that I had finally gone to see a doctor for it. Which is when I found out that I would've started experiencing this pain around the same time period no matter what.

One of these busy days on the production floor, about a month into my employment, a good friend of mine had approached me. I had known him before I started working there because he was one of my best friends' brothers and later became one of my best friends himself. He had taken the day before off on vacation because he had gone to the dentist. I can't remember what procedure he had said that he went through. All I remember was that they had given him narcotics for the pain. He pulled me aside and handed me a pill with a huge grin and said to take it as soon as I could. He told me that this was going to make me feel much better. So, being that he had never lied to me before, I did. At first I thought that he was just screwing with me or something. I mean nothing was different at all. After about ten to fifteen minutes, I was in a great mood, but nothing that I hadn't known before. I was just being me and screwing around. I liked to make work a little more fun by being weird. About a half hour into this is when I realized that I was no longer familiar with this feeling. This was new to me. Everything seemed better. My mood. My back pain. My day. Everything, and I mean everything, seemed to just be better. And that was when I had fallen in love with Vicodin.

I feel that I should point something out to anybody that hasn't tried this before or doesn't know what I am talking about firsthand. Vicodin is a perfectly viable way to manage pain. I am in no way saying that this medicine is bad. Those that actually need it, should be able to take it. There is just a certain risk to taking it that doctors were not explaining at that time. That feeling that I described, the experience that I just told you about, is exactly why this can very well be a dangerous drug. I mean if you were to experience this and you didn't get any warning, wouldn't you want to keep it going? That is a perfectly natural feeling and one that millions struggle with the world over every single day.

If you find yourself in a situation where you actually need this, there are some things that you can do to avoid waking up this beast that we call addiction. First of all, never let yourself take it by yourself. I do not mean that you should be using with someone else. Not at all. But someone else should have knowledge of your prescription. Ideally, this person should be someone that you would trust to hold on to it for you, without taking any themselves. And remember, just because they don't actually use them, does not mean that they won't take any because there is always that chance that they steal some and either give them to someone else, or they sell them to make a little extra money

Also, please remember that most doctors will actually call you in for a pill count. They will figure out how many you should have taken (using number of days multiplied by dosage) by the date that you are called in for it, and if you have a different amount, there are consequences. There is a little bit of wiggle room there, but it's only a couple usually. By that I mean if you accidentally skipped a dose on one day, it will probably show up during this count. That is typically okay. If you have too many, usually the doctor will address this with the patient to find out why there's extra. If there are not enough, the doctor will usually also address this. However, in that case, the police may become involved. In most cases, the doctor will investigate and proceed accordingly, which is normally to just stop the prescription.

If you plan it out, you can definitely keep yourself (and others) safe. There are safe guards that can be used, as you can see. Just remember that you have to use them responsibly.

After the effects had worn off, I knew that I wanted more. It just made me feel better than I ever had. I felt like I could do anything I wanted to. I felt like I could take on the world and still be in perfect shape. In fact, if it wasn't for my friend warning me against telling anybody at all about this incident, I would have shouted it from the rooftops. This was just such an amazing experience to me that I had to get to that point again.

So I went looking for my friend again. Once I found him, he did wind up giving me a couple more of them. However, he warned me that he wouldn't be able to help me out with it anymore for a little while. I think I had given him something like five dollars. I don't know. All I remember was that I loved every minute of it.

Soon after that, I was off and running. I was looking for anyone and anywhere that would help feed my habit. If there was anybody that I had found out had gone in for surgery or had been to the hospital due to injury, I made sure to meet up with them. Usually I used the almighty dollar to get what I wanted, and I made sure to never steal for them. I used that as an excuse to convince myself that I was not an addict.

When I started working at this factory, I had also picked up another bad habit. When I had gotten my first paycheck, some of my coworkers had invited me to a bar. It was really run down and typical of what I would have imagined if somebody told me about a "hole-in-the-wall" bar. There was plenty of drinking, gambling, and fighting. All three of which can be considered addictions in their own right. This quickly turned into almost like a second home for me. It turned out to also be a hotspot for the workers at the factory on payday because they were known to cash paychecks for three dollars per check.

Almost every night you could find me there after I got off of work. My shift ended at 11:00 every night so usually by 11:15 p.m. I could be found holding down one of their barstools. I was there so frequently that it became common place to pull me behind the bar on busier nights to help the staff serve. I had even talked them into opening up on Sundays for a short amount of time. I absolutely loved the atmosphere and quickly memorized every song on the jukebox. My nights were indefinitely planned out for what I thought would be the rest of my life. The only time I would differ from this schedule was when I started playing poker on Thursday nights. Outside of that, I could be found at the bar. And the only problem that I saw was the one thing that I kept hidden for as long as possible. I was only eighteen years old when I started going there.

Now I'm sure that you would expect me to write about some undercover police officer coming in and busting the bar for serving me, or arresting me and carting me off to jail. Fortunately for me, that never happened. At least not there. I did, however, get my first DUI after one of those nights. I had just finished off yet another long night at the bar and decided that I wanted to grab a case of Mountain Dew on my way home. If I would have gone straight home, I would've taken the same backroads that I always had to avoid any of the police seeing me. However, that night I had to take a main state route because that was the only way to get to a store. The worse part about getting pulled over was that it wasn't for my driving. It was because as I was pulling into the parking lot of the store, the officer on duty had spotted that one of my headlights was blown out, so he turned his lights on as I was pulling in and parked behind me in the parking lot. It was so incredibly surreal to me because I had thought that there was absolutely no way that this could happen to me. I thought that I would never get pulled over with a DUI. Which is a thought that seems to be in common with everybody that gets their first DUI. Sometimes it's what they think all of the time.

That should have been a wakeup call for me (Are you keeping count of how many there are?), but yet again I was more concerned with just not getting caught. I mean, at first I actually did try to be good. If I went to the bar, I would find a ride there and back, or I wouldn't drink. Then I started testing the waters again with controlled drinking. By that I mean that I would have one or two, and then wait for a couple of hours afterward before I left. I should point out that both methods are perfectly viable ways to keep from getting in trouble. If you choose to go with the drink and wait method, please remember that it is about one hour per drink that you've had, and I would recommend an extra hour on top of that. If you choose to tempt fate with one of these, I wish you the best of luck and make sure that you can stick to them strictly. No leaving before the times up. However, if you do not know whether or not you can stick to this, I recommend not even trying because you, my friend, may very well be an addict. And if you are, there is no shame in it.

# CHAPTER 7

◆ ◆ ◆

Eventually, I was back to full on drinking and partying at the bar. I was even finding new reasons to go. I would go to compete in pool tournaments, in which I was actually rather good. I would go to meet up with others to play poker or other card games in the back corner. I even started using a bunch of my music equipment to start DJing. I just felt like I was finally home. It was like everybody actually liked to be around me when I was there, despite the fact that I'm sure that was far from the truth. It was just like that show Cheers. Everybody knew my name.

About a year into my employment with Kraftmaid, I had decided that I needed a new project. From the time that I had learned the basics of guitar, I was constantly trying to find bands to join. On the last failed attempt that I had joined, I had looked at some of the other members that had either been recently kicked out or were currently with the group and unhappy with it, and decided that I would just try creating my own. Therefore, my friend Chris and I had gotten together and formed our first band. I had taught him some of the guitar and I was sick of playing instruments because I had played each one of them at least once each in various failed projects. Therefore, Chris was to be the guitarist and I took vocals.

Starting up what was later named Sunless Dawn seemed impossible for a little while because Chris and I couldn't seem to get up and do anything about it. However, soon I received a call from Jake, a friend from school and one of the guitarists from the last band that I was in. He had left and wanted to try joining with us after he had heard that we were trying to form something. Right off rip he had conditions. Two of them actually. First of all, we had to try to use a riff that he had recently written. That one was easy because it wasn't bad at all. I was definitely able to come up with something. His second condition was that Chris and I switch places. He wanted me in the rhythm guitar spot and Chris on vocals. This took a little convincing on his part, but eventually I caved. I figured that despite the lack of a challenge, which is what I was kind of looking forward to, at least this was more in my wheelhouse than vocals were.

Shortly thereafter, we were able to recruit my good friend Jon on the bass. He was another member of the other band that we had come from. However, he had intended to do both. We agreed to that because it didn't make a difference to me. Plus, I felt like it was just a matter of time before that band split anyway. And it turned out that I was right.

Drums was a little more of a challenge than the other members. Guitarists and bassists were a dime a dozen around the area, but drummers were kind of few and far between. Especially drummers that shared the same vision as us. After what seemed like forever, we had finally found one. I had been friends with him for quite a while, however, I had never known that he played anything, much less any kind of drum. So we asked him to try out and he agreed. This initiated a whole new period of waiting. Every week we would have practice in the makeshift studio that I had created in the basement of my parents' house, and every week my friend would tell us that he needed help digging his set out of his garage. In hind sight, this probably should have been a red flag, but I was staying consistently high, so I never really noticed the flag.

After about a month of this, I had decided that I had enough of this. So I took another one of my music store trips and bought a brand new set. That way, when my friend showed up to practice empty-handed, there would be a brand new set already set-up and waiting for him. I kind of expected that now that I had bought this set, he would coincidentally show up with his set in the car. Fortunately he had not.

By then we had already written three or four complete songs worth of material and my friend had heard each one in practices past, so we knew that he was familiar with it. We decided on one to try him out on and started. As soon as my friend started playing, I felt like I had made a mistake by extending the invitation. Now he was definitely talented with the drums and he had plenty of skill, but there was no connection that I could make in my head between his drumming and our music. It sounded almost like he was playing in a high school marching band to me. Was he playing actual marching band parts? I really don't think so. And he was trying hard to get that connection, it just wasn't working out. He saw the look on my face and asked me what was wrong. "I just have a feeling that everything will be better next week," is how I replied. That was it. Thinking back now, I really should have been more honest with him about it and told him right away that he wasn't working out, But for some reason, I felt like this approach was better.

No sooner did my friend leave, when Jake asked me a question that I really wasn't expecting. He looked at me and said "So Ryan. Do you still know how to keep a beat on those things?" In the past, I was known to learn every instrument that I could get my hands on. So he had already known that I was able to do at least basic drumming. However, I didn't have nearly enough experience to do that full time. But that was okay. The plan that Jake had been formulating didn't necessarily require a lot of drumming experience. It was pretty simple. He wanted me to get behind the drums to keep a drum part going for the songs while he played more rhythm guitar, for the most part. Then in the meantime, we would continue to look for a drummer so that I could switch back. At least that was supposed to be the plan.

A few weeks into this, Jake came to practice with a surprise guest. Dave, who was my oldest friend because he was the first person I had met in school when I moved to Orwell. And in Dave's hand was a suspicious, long case with a handle. Of course, I had identified it instantly, as many people would. It's not difficult to spot a guitar case.

Three guitarists? What was Jake's angle hear? Was Dave just here to jam out a little bit? And when were we going to finally find a drummer? I had even started drafting wanted ads for the classifieds. It only took me slightly longer to figure out what Jake's plan was here. I have a feeling that you have already figured it out though, because by the end of the day that day, I had become the official drummer. At least there was the challenge that I was looking for in the beginning of this musical journey. And honestly, by the next day, I really didn't mind.

We weren't sounding bad at all so far. However, we had only instruments and needed someone to compliment Chris's voice, as he really wasn't covering all of the tonal ground that we needed. Which is where my brother entered the scene. We needed the primal tone that he brought. The sheer anger that came from him was outstanding. And in every way, he was the party scene, which most might see as a bad thing when you're trying to get something like this off of the ground. But what most don't think of is the positive from this. Mike was always the guy that people went to if they were looking to party and he was also known for representing the local metal scene in it's entirety. Therefore, he knew how to market our sound to this scene. He

43

knew how to get the crowds moving, and in that regard never disappointed. With him, we felt like it was time to get to work. We felt like we were unstoppable.

Now there is something else that you should know about Mike before I go on. We are only 18 months apart, so we grew up together. We were always only a grade apart and during my early childhood, he was my best friend. In fact, at times, he was my only friend. We have had our differences and fought with each other like siblings tend to do, but I definitely love the guy. Despite what he has done, I am proud of him for some of the things he has done, like becoming the absolutely phenomenal artist that he is and following his dream of becoming a tattoo artist, getting out there, and accomplishing it. He has his demons to get over, just like I have mine. So please understand that if I mention him in this book and it seems to be in a negative light, even just slightly, it's not meant to be a jab at him. It's just what happened. Mike, if you're reading this, I love you man, I'm here for you whenever I can be, and I am proud of the positive things that you have accomplished.

With all of that being said, we were off to the races. Yet we hit a snag. We weren't making enough progress. We had gotten to the point that we were playing shows, but that was it. To me, that was enough for now. Given that I had never been so nervous in my life than the day of my first performance. We were playing at a graduation party for Chris's younger sister and as far as I'm concerned, we bombed it. Badly. Everything that we tried to play, we had somehow completely screwed up. We had started off bombing so badly that we had to stop three songs in to regroup. After that point though, we were back. It was weird really because when we started back up, we played better than we ever had. I couldn't believe my ears.

After that performance, I was high. This is one of the only

times in this book that I will refer to being high and it's not in a negative context or a result of using any drugs. Actually, the high that came from playing a show has always been, and will always be, my favorite feeling in the world. I have said it several times and I will say it many more, the high that I got from playing a show is the best high that I have ever felt in my life, despite the different highs that I have experienced from the many different drugs that I have done.

We were ready to just keep going. We had started playing more really small shows around the county. I still remember one of my favorites being the talent show at our town's local fair. At the very last minute we had decided to enter and I vividly remember playing our song in front of the town, the town actually cheering for us (despite losing the contest), and packing up to get out of there. While we were packing up, a couple of kids that had to have been in elementary school grades approached me with matching grins. They had asked me to sign something (I can't remember what to save my life). I was taken off guard with this request because I had never been asked that. I of course agreed to do so and while I was signing, one of the kids looked at me and told me that I was the best drummer in the world. Given that I was never anywhere near being even the best drummer in the county, I still remember that comment to this day because it meant more to me than the autographs did to them. For the first time I really felt like I was going to actually be somebody.

During another show that we had performed, we had gotten a spot at the very same bar that I had spent so much time in while working for Kraftmaid. I'm pretty sure this was also the only show that my mom had ever gone to. I remember walking through the crowd and finding her, heading away from the bar with her arms completely full of different beers. The sight made me laugh out loud because I had never seen her drink even one beer and here she was carrying six. She then proceeded to hand out one to each of the band members. The thought of her doing this still makes me laugh, but she just wanted to show us support. I don't know if she just figured that nobody would be there to support us or what, but she was definitely there.

We definitely did not have a problem with a supportive turn out that night either. That was honestly the first time that I had felt like I was succeeding. We started with our normal routine. Get to the venue, unpack the equipment, set up, and then enjoy a little down time while we got our head space right. During that last part, I had gone up to the bar to grab a beer. Afterward, I got to thinking. We had no tickets for this show because it was at a hole-in-the-wall bar. I don't remember even having a cover charge at the door. I'm pretty sure that we were just letting people in and partying with them. So I had no way of knowing how many people were actually there. So after I had gotten my beer I took a quick swig and set it down by my drum set. In the back, there was a door off to the side that led outside, just in case there was an emergency. For the hell of it, I decided to step out there to get a look at how many cars were there. The bar was already getting pretty full, so I had expected to see a decent turnout. What I hadn't expected was what I had actually seen.

When I stepped through the door, I thought for sure that I was dreaming. There was a line from the front door, all the way to the road, which is where it kind of kinked over to make rom for a handful of people more. I couldn't believe what I was seeing. Like we could have been staring down the barrel of a serious capacity issue. And if that wasn't enough, some of the waiting spectators saw me standing there and approached me with all kinds of different items. At first I was confused, but it became obvious really quickly what they wanted. These people wanted autographs! From me of all people! It turned out that these people had either already heard us or had heard enough about us that they felt like we were going to be huge and they wanted autographs at the ground level just in case. I actually felt like a somebody, and I wanted more.

We booked several shows at clubs in Cleveland, Youngstown, and other much smaller places. Now it was time to tweak our group for the sake of success. After all, we were trying to do this to become huge.

I still can't remember exactly how we reached this decision. It's kind of a blur here. I only remember that it was a bittersweet conclusion that turned out to be a whole lot more bitter than sweet over time. Somehow or another, we had reached the decision to boot Chris. I felt like we could work with him still, his voice just didn't fit at the moment. I remember telling him a few different times to change this or that about other aspects at our shows. For example, we played a show in Cleveland one night and when I looked up, Chris had brought his little brother up on stage. Now by itself, that really wasn't a problem. Actually, I am friends with his little brother to this day. However, this was a show that people had paid for, so I had to explain to him that those people had paid to see our show, not to see other fans on stage. I know that it sounds kind of ridiculous now, but that really is the case. After that, we had no more problems like that.

However we had come to this decision to kick Chris out, I do remember feeling like an absolute scumbag for it. And almost as quickly as he had gone, a replacement came in to try out. This was my first experience with Ron.

# CHAPTER 8

◆ ◆ ◆

Ron was a pretty cool guy himself. I mean, we all got along with him and he could sing. It seemed like we were having our luck change for the better. Now for the problem though. It turned out that he partied just as much as me and Mike. Looking back, this should have been a huge red flag that we needed to change something and quickly, but we were having way too much fun.

I'm pretty sure that Jake had brought him in. Apparently he had also auditioned for one of those singing shows, which we thought had to mean something. In hindsight, anybody could audition for those shows. It's not like he had won or anything.

However, he was able to sing, which was what we were missing at that moment. You see, Chris wasn't able to sing as well. He could write lyrics. In fact, he was pretty damn good at writing songs. It's just that he couldn't actually sing. Ron, however, seemed to be the opposite in this regard. He could sing really well. As for writing, not quite so good. But we'll get into that a little later. For now, let's just say at least he was able to sing well. Plus, we all got along with him.

I still see Ron from time to time, when I'm walking around on the strip in Geneva, Ohio or in a random store from time to time. I've always liked the guy. And as for the band, he complimented Mike's style really well. So it was time to hit the studio, as in an actual studio.

While Mike was fully immersed in the Cleveland local metal scene, he had made a lot of different friends. Amongst those, he was able to introduce me to a band that I find myself getting their songs stuck in my head to this day. They went by the Junkie Massacre X-Periment they were made up of some of the coolest people I have ever met, not to mention the raw talent that these guys had. It was insane to me I was even regularly hanging out with these people. They weren't famous by any stretch of the imagination, by they really should have been.

The front man for this group was probably the one that I related to the most. He went by Sinner (and because I respect him, I refuse to share his actual name) and he happened to have his own recording studio. From what I understand, this studio was put together a lot like mine. The big difference, Sinner had some top-of-the-line equipment on hand. I'm talking the huge sound boards, an isolated vocal booth, the expensive microphones, and so much more. With him being behind the board, I felt like we had to wind up with a hit album because he really knew his stuff, which is why I related to him so much. In Sunless Dawn, I was the one that was always working on the music and operating the equipment. I'm not sure why we were accepted into Sinner's studio or whether anybody was even paying for our sessions, but I wasn't about to question it. It already felt like I had made it.

This wound up becoming a three day long project and we were only doing four songs. First up was the drum tracks so that everybody else would at least have a beat to work with. This should have gone smoothly considering that I had never missed a cue since that first show. However, nothing could be further from the truth. If I remember correctly, my parts took the entire first day. That day I had decided to get high, as I usually did, before-

hand. A couple of the pills that I was taking were actually uniden-
tified and I was just trying them out because I didn't have much of
my beloved pain killers.

Everything had started out all right, but that didn't last
long. About halfway through our first song, I started feeling really
strange. My heart was beating way too fast. I was extremely
shaky. I could not focus on anything to save my life. So, because
of all of this, I was unable to get anything done in the first half of
the time that we were there. And being that there were no com-
pleted drum tracks, nobody else could get anything done either.
I had cost the band some valuable recording time and, although I
was at least a little scared for my life during that whole ordeal, I
was only worried about getting high again.

After I had gotten through that, the rest of our time in
the studio was pretty smooth. We hit a small rough patch with
recording one of the guitar solos and both vocalists had to do
several takes on all four songs before we got it close enough to
perfect, but all and all it was kind of uneventful. We would record
a couple of member's parts on each song and then spend a couple
of hours hanging out with whatever other musicians stopped by
during the process. We also spent a whole lot of the time just jamming together, which was probably my favorite part of the whole
experience.

After we had finally finished with all of our tracks, each
member got a copy. We were instructed to take it to get it rep-
licated (as opposed to duplicated) somewhere and then we went
on our way. We never did get any replications done, but oh well
because if we had actually made it anywhere in the music indus-
try, it would have probably been the death of me. This was the
first professional demo that we had ever done. It was also the last
professional demo that we had ever done because it was all down
hill from here.

We continued to play plenty of shows. However, we stopped doing Cleveland shows as much, which tapered off pretty quickly, and started doing more local shows than anything. Especially at one local bar to Middlefield, Ohio that was simply named The Patio Tavern. In an attempt to make some extra money, I had begun taking all of my music equipment to bars to DJ. It was a great way to make a little extra money, plus either the bars gave me free beers or the customers would continue to buy them for me. I was just turning any bar that I went to into one big party.

It started with me just having some fun at a local bar in Orwell called Creekside Inn. For one reason or another, their DJ had up and left. However, the bar owned the mixers, speakers, etc. so I would bring my CD's in and just play around with them in the back of the bar. People typically loved it, so I would just keep going and started to do this every night. By this time I had turned 21 already (when the head bartender in my usual bar found that out, she freaked because she hadn't realized that I had started when I was 18) so I wasn't going to any bars as often as I used to. For some reason I essentially stopped going after about a month of being 21. It was like the novelty had worn off. But now I had a new reason to start ramping it up again.

After a while of this going on, I had convinced my friend into trying to get a replacement DJ. I figured that I would be an absolute shoo in for this because I was known for doing precisely that already. My friend's mother also happened to be a good friend of the bar's owner. I still remember coming in and finally getting the verdict for this decision. I had stopped in to go screwing around with the equipment again and my friend was already there. When he saw me, he had a smile on his face, but at the same time he looked kind of uneasy. Almost fidgety. I should've known something was wrong right then. He approached me and let me know that he had both really good news and really bad news. The really good news was that the owner loved the idea of having a DJ come in again. He thought that would really help out with sales. However, the really bad news kind of caught me off guard. Not only were they not going to be extending me the offer, but they had already extended the offer to my friend instead. Even better, he had already accepted.

I honestly didn't know how to react. I was severely angry because I couldn't shake the feeling that my friend had taken this job right out from under me. But I couldn't act on that feeling because I was also happy for him for at the very least finding a job that he actually liked. Since this happened, I have stopped in to hang out with him while he works this job. Since that day my friend has upgraded his equipment and expanded to another bar. I'm actually impressed because he's really doing this well and as a DJ, he's also really good. So being that I didn't know what to do with this information, I simply drank. Heavily.

When I say that I drank heavily, please understand that I'm not entirely sure why. I have had way worse happen to me than this so I'm not sure what I was thinking. Honestly, I think that I only drank heavily because that's what I knew, and this was just another perfect excuse. I mean, this was my normal pattern already. Every time that I had a great day, I found the need to celebrate with drinking and drugs. Every time that I had a horrible day, well didn't you hear? You just have to make it better with drinking. And drugs. I had already started to notice this, but I ignored it because I just didn't want to admit to a problem. Plus, everybody did this, right?

I quickly decided that I was going to just find another venue. So one of my good friends came out and picked me up and we went bar hopping. This was still kind of different from the bar hopping that I usually did because at each place I would have no more than one drink, if I had any. My main purpose was to try to find a new place to DJ on the weekends. Luckily, my disease hadn't gotten bad enough that I had lost sight of that. After about four or five places, I finally found one that would give me a shot. It was my first time meeting who we called "Mr. Rogers" (He really reminded us of him with the way that he dressed and acted) and he happened to own a really small bar called the Patio Tavern (The same Patio Tavern that I had mentioned earlier).

# CHAPTER 9

◆ ◆ ◆

This was only slightly different than Creekside in that it was much smaller and they didn't have the equipment for me to use. Therefore, I just patched it all together with the equipment that I already had in my studio. Every week or so, the owner had cover bands that would come through to jam out and as a DJ, he had offered the breaks to me. So when the band would stop for a little while, I was on for a half an hour or so. Then I would also close out the nights after they were completely done with their set. It was the perfect job for me. Drink, hang out, and listen to plenty of music, both live and recorded. The only thing that was missing was me being able to play as well. A situation that was remedied shortly thereafter.

On the second or third gig that I had while doing this, some of the other band members started showing up. And after that, they started bringing some of our fans with. Before I knew what was happening, we had booked a show there as well. You should know that before Sunless Dawn descended upon this little bar, the tone was a bit different. By that I mean the bands that played there when I was just DJing all played classic rock, with maybe a little 80's hair metal. They all looked like fathers and grand-fathers, and the patrons were the kind that would just sit around at the bar. During the show, you might see a few people stand-ing up, a few sitting down. Most could still be found at the bar. The bands were there just because these people loved to just jam, whether people were watching or not. I wish I remembered some of their names because I had met a lot of really cool musicians and they disappeared just as quickly as I had met them. But then it happened. Sunless Dawn came in and flipped that bar on it's side. There goes the neighborhood.

Being that this was a small bar, it was fairly easy to completely pack it. Our first show there had been a huge success, therefore offered to have us come back. He also asked us to bring more bands with us. Before we knew it, we had essentially turned this tiny bar into an actual venue. There were shows being performed almost every weekend. The sales there increased drastically. Actually, now that I think about it, I have no idea why they had shut the doors and if you were to go through Middlefield today, you would see that the bar was torn down and now there's a Taco Bell.

Every show that we performed had gotten rowdy. The audience would demand an encore every time and every time we would get cut short during our extra set because somebody had gotten hurt or into a fight. And after we would get shut down, the owner of the bar would approach us, grinning from ear to ear, and tell us how great he thought we sounded that night, how he thought that we put on a great show, and how much he wanted to see us back soon. It was absolutely amazing. We were having the time of our lives.

The entire time I had been doing my share of drugs. And by that I mean that I would do any drug that I could find. I was spiraling out of control, and honestly, it felt like I was actually sailing pretty smoothly. I had no idea what to expect.

During the entire Sunless Dawn experience, I was out of my mind and thought that everybody else was crazy. I don't mean that literally, but it's as close as I can get to describing it. I was constantly on some kind of pain killer, or anti-anxiety pill, or muscle relaxer. I was also finding more things to get into that I would mix with this stuff. I would do these almost in trends. The first time that I had ventured into harder drugs, I found that I absolutely loved cocaine. It would speed me up to the point that I felt like I could get anything and everything done. And of course, I did this in absolute excess.

I had tried to deal coke as well. I would get an amount fronted to me, and then sell it, get the money to my dealer, and get some more. The biggest problem with this, I was using it almost as fast as I was selling it. So my first go-round with this new plan of mine, I made absolutely nothing. I had broken even and just barely had enough to pay my dealer back. The second time, I made absolutely nothing. When I spoke to my dealer, he was not happy, but he did give me some time to come up with the money. The day that I did, he had actually shown up at my apartment. I told him that I was surprised to find him at my door but glad at the same time because I had his money. His reply was that he was very relieved because he had shown up to either collect or beat a lesson into me. Needless to say, that was the last time that I tried to do that.

# CHAPTER 10

◆ ◆ ◆

I had met quite a few interesting people while I was still partying. I remember one that we simply called Binary. I'm keeping his actual name out of here because I haven't gotten his permission to include it in this book and, to be honest, I really don't even know it. He was an interesting person himself, not to mention he had plenty of money. I don't know why he had that much money or how he came into it because I didn't ask for two different reasons. First of all, that was none of my business and I make a point not to pry. And secondly, why should I care? I mean he was coming by with massive amounts of cocaine and acid, all for personal use. With me. There was no reason to even worry about it.

When he came over, my brother and I knew that we were going to have a hell of a time. Most of these times we would just lock ourselves in my apartment and proceed to get higher than we ever have before. Then we would sit around and talk all night long while we played strategy games, such as chess. I know. I did read that back to myself. We weren't exactly going crazy. But at the same time, while we were on that stuff, we were going out of our minds. When he would bring over acid, we would just stare off at everything we could because, obviously, we were seeing all kinds of weird things like my cabinets melting or water washing over my very dry, very dirty floor.

We kept this up for quite a while and had a method to it. Whenever our friend would come out, which was actually pretty frequently, we would go buy some kind of narcotic like oxycodone or Vicodin. Something like that. We called that our "landing gear". Then after we were done "flying" for the night/day, we would revert to our landing gear to keep us from "crashing" uncontrollably. If you have ever been on cocaine, you know what I am talking about. When you come down off of that high, it thoroughly sucks. you get really jittery and antsy. You can't seem to think straight at all. You just feel like absolute shit. What goes up must come down. And for every action, there is an equal and opposite reaction. Both of these apply here because if you get yourself that high, you are going to feel equally low when it wears away.

Imagine, if you will, being able to take something so that every ounce of happiness that you can potentially feel hits you all at once. Everything that makes you happy just happens. You would be on Cloud Nine, right? Everything would feel amazing. You would easily be able to convince yourself that you have essentially won at life, if that was actually possible. Now what happens when all of that happiness dissolves? As I said, you have just experienced all of the happiness that you could have potentially felt. How do you feel when all of the happiness is gone? I know that this is really an abstract view on it and it might be kind of difficult to wrap your head around it, but it's accurate. Actually, it might be hard to wrap your head around it, if you have never been an addict. However, to us, this is very much a reality. Or at least it was during our respective times.

My cocaine habit eventually evolved into a crack habit. It would get me to hit a point that was ten times higher than cocaine ever had. The tradeoff? The low point was equally as low. But at the time I didn't care at all. I was happy to do so because of that initial feeling I went through all of my money within a week and just kept going. I was also trying to push myself to my limits with it. I would break off bigger and bigger chunks to put in the pipe at one time. Actually, I remember on a few occasions telling someone that my goal was to get myself to throw up because to do so, you had to be really high. The problem (outside of the fact that being a crack addict was terrible in every way as is) was that you can only really do that with the first hit, when your tolerance is near nonexistent. After that, it's just called chasing the dragon, and you will never catch it. I already knew all of this, but that didn't stop me from trying every chance that I got. I wanted that first hit all of the time.

I think it was my second time using crack (abuse would imply that there is a normal way to use. There is not) that I had found out that I didn't mind throwing up while I was high. I found this out when I started to wrap my head around how relative the size of the chunk was to the level of being high. The first hit that I took was a "boulder" and for the first five minutes afterward, I felt higher than I had ever felt before. I had passed Cloud Nine way up in the first three minutes. Now let's look at the chemical reaction with the human body. Crack is a much stronger version of cocaine, which is already an extreme upper (meaning that it speeds you up, if you didn't already know). With it being so much stronger, it speeds you up way past what the cocaine form can do. With that kind of increase in speed comes a drastic increase in metabolism. And with that comes a sudden feeling of nausea. In this case, this was enough to make me hurl. However, this differed from most other times in that I almost enjoyed it. And the feeling afterward was still phenomenal. It was just normal to me, yet so very abnormal to the rest of the world.

I was heading down in yet another spiral. And worse yet, I couldn't see it. And even worse, everybody else could. People cut ties with me at an alarming rate. My mother actually disowned me for about a week. And that should speak volumes because my mother does not just walk away. She isn't wired like that. She is wired to overachieve (as much as I know she does not want to admit it and when she reads this she will probably be shaking her head while saying out loud "I'm not an overachiever," Mom. You are That's a good thing. Might as well admit it.) and she will try everything in her power to fix what she sees as wrong before giving up. That means that I was beyond her help. In fact, at that point, there was only one person that could help me. And I despised the guy.

She did try to fix me, as I knew that she would. I remember that last attempt very vividly. In fact, I remember it so vividly, it feels like it was literally just yesterday. It was a Tuesday morning. By morning I mean late morning. Like 11:00 or so. The sky was completely covered with dark clouds and the rain had been coming down for hours. By this point it had let up to a light trickle. My parents had a red Ford truck that they drove around, which had virtually none of the options offered at the dealership. My mom showed up and shot me a text. I had been up all night, smoking crack with a couple of friends that I will leave nameless here (that is their story to tell). The text from my mom was short and to the point. "I'm parked outside in the parking lot. Come out here now." For the record, I'm paraphrasing that text just because I can't remember word-for-word of what it said. I freaked out for a second because I didn't want to be around her. In fact, anybody that is high doesn't want to be around their parents. If they do, chances are they are getting high too.

I stuck my head out of the entrance for the apartment building that I was living in, spotted the truck, and ran over. I tried to just talk from outside of her window, but she had shut that idea down immediately so I had to hop into the passenger seat. The talk really never stuck in my mind, but the gist of it was "Ryan, you need help. Badly. And if you don't get help really soon, you will either be locked up or dead." Of course I wasn't listening because I didn't see anything wrong with what I was doing. At the same time though, I knew enough that I was hiding all of it from anybody and everybody. I remember trying to tell her that I was absolutely fine and that there was no reason to worry about me. I couldn't figure out why she wouldn't believe me. Well, actually I couldn't figure it out on my own. She pointed out how the pipe burn was obvious on my lips.

When I wouldn't comply with what she wanted, she told me that although she didn't want to, she had to cut me loose. It was hard enough on her when my sister died. So for the next week I was essentially disowned. I didn't hear from my parents and they didn't hear from me. I continued to do the same exact things that I had just swore up and down that I wasn't. I remember that much. The rest or the specifics, however, were a blur. I also vividly remember my father's visit. He knocked on my door and I yelled to come on in. It was the middle of the day at the time, but I was laying down on my couch to get some sleep. He told me to just stay put because it would be easier on both of us, as I was facing the back of the couch. He proceeded to talk to me about the impact that I was having on the family, on him, on my mother, and of course on my health. He also saw where this was taking me and knew that I hadn't been arrested for it at all. He knew that I was getting away with it legally, therefore, chances are I was going to die instead of seeing the inside of any jail. All he really made sure to tell me was how much he loved me, how much he cared, and how he felt about it all. This time we both cried. I had really felt this one.

# CHAPTER 11

◆ ◆ ◆

After he had left, I started actually thinking this through for the first time ever. I continued to use drugs for a little while, but not as heavily and this was very short lived. I was going to be getting evicted soon and I didn't know what to do, so I reached out to my parents. They allowed me to come back, but only if I agreed to go to AA meetings. Given that I was not an alcoholic, it was really the only help that I could get locally. At least the only help that I could get without health insurance or money at all. I agreed, and not as reluctantly as I had thought that I would. Honestly, deep down, I just wanted to be done suffering.

I remember my first meeting well. It was a Monday night in a small town called Windsor, Ohio. It was held in the basement of some little old church, and the church was ironically located right next to the town bar. Often I thought about getting dropped off for the meeting and just walking over to the bar to kill the next hour. Given that I would have never gotten away with it because my mother has the nose of a blood hound, I just couldn't help but have this fantasy.

It was an open lead meeting, which means that anybody could attend and the bulk of the meeting was going to be someone telling their story, a condensed version of what I'm doing right now in a way. The speaker is to tell everybody what it was like, what happened, and what it is like today. That is a direct quote when I asked what a lead was. After the lead is finished, everybody gets a chance to stand and comment on the lead if they want to. I'm of course leaving out the prayers and readings, but those really only take up a small amount of time. I was definitely already expecting to hear all of this, from the prayers to the comments and everything in between. There really was no surprise to it. The real surprise to me kind of blind-sided me. I really hadn't expected that I would enjoy it as much as I did.

I found that the people that I found at these meetings were wonderful and supportive. Even to a complete stranger like myself. I started to go every night from that point on. I don't think that I really had ever introduced myself in any of these meetings. After about a week I began experiencing the pink cloud. If you are not familiar with this term, let me explain.

Once someone gets clean and sober, things tend to start to fall into place for them. People start to trust them. They start to enjoy the little things in life. And everything seems to be perfect, or as close to perfect as they ever have been before, giving the person a feeling like they are almost floating on a cloud. To most, they report that it is like they are on, and I quote, a "pink cloud." This has gone on to be labeled as the pink cloud phenomena. The other thing you should know about the pink cloud phenomena is that it can be extremely dangerous to those that are not expecting it, and also some people that are.

It sounds like this is the feeling that you would want. I mean, who wouldn't want to feel like they're simply floating along on a cloud, regardless of color? The problem though, lies in the sense of security that comes with it. It makes you feel like you are doing great. Like you can handle this no matter what. But it's easy to stay clean and sober when you have everything falling into place. It's easy when things are going your way to say no or avoid a drink or a drug entirely. But what happens when something does go wrong (and it certainly will)? When everything starts to go askew, will you still be able to stay in the right frame of mind? Can you drive past that bar when you have an issue gnawing at you? Can you say no to your friends when your girlfriend decides that you aren't the one for her? Or when you are facing eviction because your hours were cut at work? Chances are, no you cannot. It gets difficult when everything begins to crumble around you. It feels like you are going through hell when that pink cloud finally gives way and you drop back to the real world. It's then that you have to lean on the other "tools of sobriety," such as a support group, a meeting, or even just some other activity to help you through any cravings that you may have.

# CHAPTER 12

◆ ◆ ◆

The first six months were surprisingly easy for me. Once the drug had completely left my system, I had started to become normal again. I was working for my parents during the day, either out in the machine shop or on the production floor. They would pay me minimum wage to do so and also let me live there again, without charging me for food or utilities. Then every night I would go to another AA meeting with either my mom or my dad. They weren't addicts in any way, they just made sure to go to show me support. After a while, I found that my dad would go just because he thoroughly enjoyed the company of these truly great people, saying things like "I almost wish that I was an alcoholic, just so I felt like I belonged in these rooms." They had told me to do 90 in 90 (90 meetings in 90 days), so I did something like 150 in 149. I slowly started building myself back up. I remember one instance where my father had commented at a meeting, stating that he had heard a strange noise in the shop while he was working in his office, and upon inspection he had found that it was me whistling, for the first time in years. I hadn't even realized that I had done so. But everything was looking up for me.

I kept this up for quite a while. Being that the vast majority of the people in these meetings were older men and women, I naturally started hanging out with the one guy that was around my age there. I started to meet up with them outside of meetings as well. However, once I did come down from that cloud, I found that I hadn't set myself up for success at all. The first hard time that I had, I went out and bought some pain killers. The thought of going back was killing me, but it was just what I knew. Being unable to decide whether or not I should make this leap backwards, I showed my best friend in the rooms. And that is when I had found out that he wasn't truly sober either because we wound up doing them together.

This started me into yet another downward spiral. I would still go to meetings, I would just go while I was high. In fact, there were several times that I would get up in the middle of it to go use the restroom and head out to my car to take another. Technically I was still more than welcome into the meetings because the only requirement is a desire to be sober. It doesn't say anywhere that you actually have to be sober to attend the meetings. Actually, that's where I met my other not-so-sober friend in the rooms. One that would go to meetings and thoroughly enjoy them, and then go home and get as drunk as he could. He would then repeat the process the next day. It was insane.

I continued my charade for about a year. But eventually, I simply stopped going. It started with missing a meeting here and there throughout each week. Within a month or two I was missing at least half of them and a month after that I only made it to one or two a week. Then I just stopped altogether. There really was no reason for me to go because I no longer had a desire to be sober. In fact, I had a strong desire to messed up out of my mind as much as possible. Every day, all day.

I would justify my use by pointing out things that I hadn't done, most of which I had done by the time this nightmare was over. For example, I was known for saying things such as "I'm not doing too bad because at least I'm not messing with something harder like cocaine." Well we already know how that one went. Then it was "It's not like I'm messing around with crack." Yeah.

That didn't go any better. "So I like oxy/pain killers? At least I'm not high on heroin like a junkie." That is, until I found out how much cheaper and effective heroin was. Then there is my absolute favorite. The one that I said more than any of the others. "I'm no junkie because junkies shoot up. At least I don't inject myself with this shit." Spoiler alert. That was the last two months of addiction for me.

Once I was back on my self-destructive path, things started sliding downhill. I mean, for a little while I was able to manage the bad with the good, but eventually it overtook my entire life. I had started to work at my parents' company to afford the rent at another small apartment that I had secured. It was at the same place as the efficiency that I had turned into Drug Central, but this time it had one bedroom. I had originally moved in after I had gotten a job at a small steel tubing manufacturing plant that was within walking distance of the apartment complex, but I lost that after one too many incidents such as sleeping on the job (while standing up no less) and grabbing other peoples' work shirts (I still don't get how that kept happening). After I was kicked out of their ranks was when I had started working at AlpTex, Inc. It wasn't much money, but I was easily able to pay the bills.

I was also able to buy more pain killers. After work, my friend and I would go looking every day and we almost always came up with something. Her husband (who was also one of my close friends) was working at another factory in Orwell so my friend would drop him off at work, then head over to pick me up and it was off to the races. We would call anybody and everybody that we knew of that had at least had some pain killers at some point in time in the past. Both of our phones were brimming with people's numbers so we were usually quite successful with this. We called it "scheming," which let's face it, is a pretty accurate description.

Typically, I would be the one to come up with money. I mean, I'm not the only one that paid. She spent quite a bit of money herself. However, when she was out, I tried as hard as I possibly could to try to come up with enough for her as well. I never did tell her that. I wasn't trying to get her to be in debt with me so I made sure that I insisted. That was one of the only things that has usually stayed true about me even in addiction. I almost always try to make sure that my friends and family got whatever I could help with. However, in this case, I was really just hurting them by helping them get high with me. But whatever. We were "living" the way we thought was worth it and nobody could tell us any differently.

# CHAPTER 13

◆ ◆ ◆

After a while, I found myself spending an inordinate amount of time with one of my more frequent dealers. I had become good friends with her boyfriend/fiancé (whatever they were) and I had also come to be good friends with her (Let's call the guy Adam and the girl Heather. These are not their actual names because this is my story. If they want everybody to read about them and know who they really are, they can write their own books). The same could be said for her sisters, her father, her step-mother, and her amazingly sweet grandma. To this day, I still see some of them around from time to time. We no longer spend a lot of time around each other, but here and there I see them and I am still friendly to them, as they are towards me.

Whenever her fiancé would wind up in jail (which didn't happen as much as I would've suspected), I would try to help out with their kids and their awesome pit bull, Chloe. I wasn't much help, but I tried to do whatever I could. Meanwhile, I was really upping the dosage on my drug habits. Being that I was getting them from her, I found that I was staying high for longer while helping. I should point out right here that this was NOT the reason that I was helping out or why I was friends with this couple. We just shared a lot of the same interests. I also want to point out that it was really only this couple that I would get anything from. Not her grandma or her sisters.

This lasted for a little while, until the day came that the two of them had a falling out. I'm not sure if there was a big fight, or he had just taken off, or what happened. What I do know is that my friend that was left with the kids behind, all of a sudden found herself doing everything on her own. I spoke to Adam every once in a while, but it was really clear that he was gone for good. He had taken the dog and left.

Heather had two jobs and two kids, so she definitely needed the help. For the most part, I was still doing my own thing. I helped when I could, but that wasn't very often at all for the time being. I started to spend a lot of time over there, but it was simply as friends. I would speak with her about anything and everything. She told me all about the horrific things that she had endured. Her now ex-fiancé used to make sure that he was either high or drunk at all times. I bring that up because when Adam was like that, apparently he became a completely different person than the one that I knew. He would become a virtual monster, beating on Heather and destroying property. After I had heard about all of this, I had decided that I was done being miserable by myself. In my head, Adam had his chance. A few of them actually because she continued to take him back. During that time, I spent a huge chunk of my time miserably depressed because I felt like I was completely alone. I felt like there was nobody out there that would want me. A depression that was only amplified by the fact that my teeth were rotting away at the same time. So what should I do here? You guessed it. While sitting next to Heather on the couch I had decided that I was done with my horrible, lonely existence, so I leaned over and before I could second guess and stop myself, I kissed her.

I am bringing this up because that kiss wound up becoming a huge factor in where I went from there. It took some convincing on my part to do so because this really wasn't something that I typically did, but in the end I did it. I had already known that the last break up that her and Adam had was the final one. That she was done with that and now she was single. For about a week she had started to see another guy. Someone who had randomly hit on her in the gas station that she had worked at had asked her out. He seemed like a nice enough guy, but I was sick of sitting back and letting everybody else find somebody to be with. Countless times I found myself falling for someone, only to swiftly be put in the friend zone. And honestly, I really don't think that guy would have worked out because he was a very straight-laced kid. Remember, this was where I got some of my pain pills. That combination could not have worked out, so I have felt very little remorse for taking her honestly.

The first month was absolutely amazing from my point of view. We were in those initial stages where everything seems perfect and both the guy and the girl are unbelievably happy. And do you know why that happens? Because the majority of the time, it shouldn't be believed. I spent most days and nights over at her apartment. I'd watch the kids if she had to go to work. And hell, that was essentially the beginning of my sex life. This wound up being the first Valentine's Day that I actually got to spend with someone and as I was heading out to a friend's place to do a drug deal with my other friend, I had stopped at the local Circle K to find something for her. I know I really couldn't have gotten cheaper than buying a gift at the local convenience store, but I was excited to actually be with someone this time and I had damn near no money. After about a month though, that's when we started having any kind of fight.

This book isn't about me and her, so I will spare you the details. We were usually fighting about, you guessed it, drugs. And as we kept going, our habits got worse and worse. After about three months of being with each other, we decided to move in together. So I left the apartment that I had just gotten the rent caught up on, and we moved to a town that had virtually no work. I would find a minimum wage job here and there, but for the most part, we were begging for what we got. If you were to visit us, we would make it look as if we were doing great though. We would hide all of our faults and put on a happy family face. The worst part was that we thought that we had everybody fooled.

We had moved at least five or six times. And that's not counting the times that we had moved into a family members house. We would go there and claim that we were only there to help them or it was just in between apartments, and we were being honest with everybody but ourselves about it. We fully intended to do just that. However, that's not what happened. We would continue to stay way past our welcome. I mean, it's difficult to move on when you can't afford anything other than your habit.

For income I had learned to tattoo, and that's exactly what I would do. Sometimes we would also sell some kind of drugs, however, that was few and far between and we usually just used it ourselves. The jobs that either of us did get, we were never able to hold for very long. Within months we would be out of work again, scrounging to stay alive, and yet we still refused to see ourselves for what we were. We saw each other that way, but never ourselves.

Within the first year of being together, we had decided to get married. I had actually proposed towards the end of the first month of us dating. Although we were engaged, I refused to let my parents know because I knew what they would have to say. In fact, that was same with both pregnancies. I just didn't want to hear what I already knew deep inside.

In August of 2011 we had stood in front of a small group of

family and friends to tie the knot. I remember heading back to our tiny apartment after the ceremony to get changed before we went to the reception. We had that just down the strip in Geneva-on-the-lake in northeast Ohio, at a small park. It had actually come together pretty nicely. I was impressed being that everything seemed to come apart at one time right beforehand, but we had some family that had pulled together to make it happen because that's what we had said that we wanted. With all of that being said, it was one of my biggest mistakes ( for both of us) because I was an absolutely horrible father and husband and she was really no different at the time.

We had moved out of there around September or October of the same year. Despite everything that we had gone through there, I actually kind of miss that little apartment. If I was single and/or I had a license and a vehicle, it would have been a great place to live, but at the time we really couldn't afford it. For someone that couldn't drive or come up with a decent reliable means of transportation, this was really the last place that anybody would want to be. It was kind of cool during the summer months because the strip came alive with people. There was a concert venue right around the corner from where we lived and several places worked with us when we didn't have any money. The community was very community-driven, as in they really worked to help each other out, and I absolutely loved that. But we really had no business being there.

The most notable part about my time living in Geneva-on-the-Lake was the one job that I had managed to find. I began working part time at a family fun center that was located at the other end of the strip. To the best of my knowledge, the couple that had hired me had no idea that I was a drug addict. They had hired me for various odds and ends jobs like small maintenance, basic landscaping, and sometimes I would cover up the many tattoos on my arms and operate some of the attractions. I was the one that would come in every week to change the oil on all of the go-karts and I was also the one that would come in once a week to do all of the mowing. To this day I credit the owner that had hired me with being one of the people that had taught me to become an adult. I still visit there from time to time and him and his wife are doing very well. I consider them friends and would do anything they needed to help them, as that's exactly what they did for me.

After we had moved, we wound up in Ashtabula, Ohio. At the time, this city was run down and washed up. It was what one would think depression and regret would look like if it was in a physical form. I absolutely hated it. I also had to stop working at Adventure Zone because I had no way of getting there and back on the days that I did work. I had become a bum almost overnight. And the worst part is that we had options, we just chose not to look for them.

By this time, her grandma had been sick and tired of us staying with her and she wanted us gone. It was the entire half of a very run down house and we were barely able to make rent most of the time. For a little while we made the inside look absolutely fantastic by going to Rent-A-Center and grabbing everything that we could find to make it look like we were even a little success-ful. That was not our conscious reason for what we had selected, however, that really was what we were going for. A brand new PS3, a huge big-screen TV, a huge couch, and the nicest end/coffee tables that we could find. Why? Because we could just make pay-ments. I'm not sure how we figured that would work out because neither of us had any money. But that is what we were thinking.

# CHAPTER 14

◆ ◆ ◆

After about a month or so, we had found an apartment that was located about a block away from Heather's grandma. This was where my past started to catch up to me. We had an issue with our previous landlord from Geneva-On-The-Lake, So I had called the police department to file a complaint. For some reason we thought that we were living very typical lives. We thought of ourselves as being the normal American family. On the phone the police quickly dismissed my concern after I had given my name and such, and I got off of the phone. I had thought that was that, but was soon proven wrong. About ten minutes later, I had gotten a call back from them. They told me that there was something that they could do for us, but we needed to file a report. So I gave them my address without thinking anything of it. That callback should have been my first warning flag.

About a half an hour later, the police arrived. Looking out the window wound up being my actual first warning flag. I watched as two Sheriff's Deputy cars, an Ashtabula City police car, and a Geneva-On-The-Lake car pulled up alongside the road. I stepped out of the house and greeted them. They asked if I was Ryan, and upon me confirming, they proceeded to put me in hand-cuffs. Apparently there was a secret indictment out for me that I was unaware of (hence secret, right?). This worried me because this was surprisingly my first trip to the jail. Once I got to the jail they went through the whole routine of processing and took me to my pod. Luckily, this was a really short trip because the judge let me out on a PR bond on the fourth day.

The court proceedings went pretty quick. They had me after sending someone to me with a wire on him. There were records of pictures, reports, and audio recordings that incriminated me. They were very careful to make sure that I didn't have a way to identify they individual that had worn the wire and turned me in. They would do things like make sure that his name never came up in the reports and cover him up in the pictures that they had taken. At least, they had tried to keep me from identifying.

The problem with this was simple. Every time that I had gone to get drugs or anything else for someone, it almost always went the same way, over and over again. However, this time was different. I didn't have to see who was being covered on the picture because I could see the background. On that particular day, I had taken an unorthodox path. I had stopped at Circle K to look for something because, well, I was pretty broke and it was the first Valentine's Day that I had ever been with someone. Therefore, I easily remembered exactly who I had been walking with that day. The ironic part is that I see this individual around now and he looks like he is still going strong with his addiction.

We would have been evicted from there a lot sooner if it wasn't for my schooling. By this time I had tried to go to college online twice. For each time, I was able to get full financial aid (this was while Sallie May was in full profit mode and handing school loans out to literally anyone). One day, I was at that run down house, stressing out about what I was going to do about money because I had nothing for rent, food, cigarettes, etc. We were beyond broke. I remember going out to the mail box and bringing in the mail. When I got inside I lightly tossed it all on to the table, announced that it was there, and continued to dig through my mind to try to come up with a plan. I was so lost in thought that I hadn't even heard my wife say that I had mail and when she got my attention I finally took the letter from her hand.

Before opening the envelope, I quickly glanced down at the return address. It was from the schools and I couldn't help but think to myself that this couldn't possibly be good news. I opened it up, only half paying attention to what I was doing. I vividly remember thinking to myself "How in the hell am I going to do this? What am I going to do for money?" We received food stamps and my wife had been receiving a little bit of money from Social Security, however, we didn't have anything from that. Once I read it though, I had to do a triple take. I couldn't believe my eyes. I was holding a check for approximately $1,500. That total may not be accurate, but it's not too far off and to me, that was the difference between screwed and being okay.

We spent the day furiously looking for somewhere that would cash this check. We finally found a motel on the other side of the city that was willing to do so. I hadn't known why I had gotten this check, but I did know that I wanted to cash it before I found out, just in case I had gotten it by mistake. I know that wasn't exactly the honest thing to do, however, we were desperate to survive. I was able to get ahold of the school a day or two later to discuss this check with them. It turns out that it wasn't a mistake at all. I just didn't know how student loans worked.

So what they did was send the school the total amount that I was approved for. After classes, materials, and books were covered, there was some leftover. That leftover was what they had sent me. Being that I had already gone there twice and I had left the first time before I could finish, they had just sent me both of them in one. Now I saw this as another reason to stay in school. I wasn't able to hang in there, but I certainly tried.

This money only lasted us a few weeks anyhow. Heather spent it as fast as I could give it to her, buying all of the clothes she could and forming a huge collection of Bath & Body Works products in our bathroom. I only spent here and there. I think the largest purchase that I had made was a PlayStation 3, which was used so it was cheaper. We had also purchased brand new cell phones (which quickly got deactivated within a couple of months or so because we couldn't afford either of them once the check was gone). Once the money had all dried up, we had to start returning the stuff. I'm pretty sure the first thing to go back was my PlayStation (I was not happy about this, but not many could tell because I was still always high).

Once we exhausted our money, it was back to being poor. We were begging for money from friends and family, somehow getting through with just enough to get by. Actually, that would imply that we had our stuff paid up to date. In reality we didn't have anything paid. We only got by in the sense that we had our day-to-day stuff. And honestly, that was purely speculation. We're talking about energy drinks and cigarettes (can't you tell how much I had my priorities straightened out?). Things like utility bills and rent almost never got paid because for the vast majority of the time, neither of us had a job.

We had lived in several places while we were together and leading up to my breaking point, all within northeast Ohio. There was Orwell for a bit, Geneva-On-The-Lake, Ashtabula, my parents' house (which was Orwell again), Heather's sister's house (in Middlefield), Troy/Hiram, and back to Middlefield to a place of our own (and our last eviction together). And it always went the same way. We would find a place that was available, scrounge up just enough to get the security deposit and first month's rent, win over the landlord by making them think that we were a great, hard-working family that was just trying to make it, start our fighting with ourselves and our neighbors, make up excuses about not paying the rent, and eventually leave before they had the chance to evict us. The only real difference was that as time went on, we would unpack less and less until finally, while living in Middlefield for the last time, we just didn't unpack anything and just slept on an air mattress in the living room. That was also the only place that we had actually gone through the eviction proceedings that I can remember. However, we could have possibly gone through the same while in Troy. I just can't remember if Heather went to that or not.

The other common thread throughout this time period was our drug use. Our abuse was getting to be more and more as time went on. We were also diving into it more and more, using different methods of getting the stuff into our bodies. I was doing tattoos out of our living room or kitchen to get money together for whatever we needed, but that usually still didn't make it. In fact, I still can't figure out how Heather always seemed to be able to get us anything and everything that we ever needed. She seemed to make money just appear from thin air. Although, I also stopped trying to figure it out. That's a time period that I really don't need to be spending too much time thinking about.

Our final method was, of course, direct injection. I found that my problem of occasionally popping pain pills had finally evolved into a full blown heroin habit by injection. I was having other people hit a vein on me while I held the belt. Once I released that belt, my new found love took me far away from the pain and the poverty. Far away from the issues that we faced and the loneliness that my wife and I dealt with together. And yes, that is actually very possible.

Here's the issue with being taken so far away from all of our woes by this method. Once the ride is over, all of those woes come screaming back and almost destroy you. You feel a pain that you could have never felt. It's almost as if your bones are being crushed from the inside out. Every single muscle that you have aches for more. And no matter what, you will always hear that voice. The voice that you've been following all along. And that god forsaken voice will always tell you the very same thing. It'll wait for all of the pain to hit what you think to be the peak, the most that you could possibly take, and then it will whisper the same exact sentence directly into your ear. "Just one more time."

I've forgotten many different timeframes in my life. I'm absolutely sure of it. However, no matter how much my memory fails me, I will always remember the last month of my abuse like it was just yesterday. I was miserable all of the time, unless I was high. Then I was marginally less miserable. I had just started shooting up heroin and I was already in love with it. We were just starting to go through the eviction process for our last place in Middlefield. Then, about two weeks into this last month, the unthinkable happened.

# CHAPTER 15

◆ ◆ ◆

We were surprised when we found the Sheriff's department on the other side of the door after we had heard the knock. We had the Department of Family Services out to our home on a few occasions before, but that was easily brushed off. We would go through a specific process the night before to get any incriminating traces of drugs out of our hair. We would do a last minute clean up of the apartment. Then we would play the perfect American family while the case worker was over. But this was different. They had never brought the Sheriff's Deputy with them before. The entire experience was just absolutely surreal.

They informed us immediately that they were here to take our children because of our drug habits. They apparently received several calls from a whole lot of people saying that we were unfit to have them and they were in danger if they stayed with us. Maybe they were. I mean, we were honestly both horrible at the time. Neither of us were fit in any sense of the word.

The time leading up to that day left me hollow. I had no feelings. I had no emotion. The drugs had figuratively dug away at everything that was in me and all that was left was a shell of who I was. On that day, for the first time in many years, that space was filled up, and quickly. But not with what and who I was. That really wouldn't make sense if that had happened during such a problem to be honest. No, I was instantly filled with anger, depression, regret, and shame. And somewhere buried deep inside of all of this, there was a yearning. A yearning for a better life. A yearning for my kids back and my family to be whole again. I just wasn't able to bring myself to do anything about it.

I remember trying to put together everything that the kids might need and I included my favorite blanket so they would have something to remember me by. I really had no idea whether I would ever get to see them again. The entire process really only took an hour or two, but it felt like it had taken all day. And then to wrap it all up, the Deputy had pulled me off to the side to let me know that they had just found a warrant for my arrest for failure to appear. In one day, my entire life had shifted and changed for the worst.

Fortunately, the deputy absolutely had a heart. He had whispered this revelation to me so that the kids didn't overhear. He then made sure to wait until after the van that had picked up the kids had left. He didn't want them to watch this. In a matter of a couple of hours, Heather was the only one left standing there. As soon as the van had pulled around the corner and made it down the road, the deputy began the arresting process. I was hand cuffed and searched. Unfortunately for me, I had just gotten done scouring the apartment and grabbing the last bit of heroin that we had. It was in a tiny paper envelope and I had put it in the small pocket of my jeans. The deputy somehow was able to locate it. I watched in horror as he started to unfold it, bits of the drug falling out of the corners as he did. I'm not sure if he just felt bad for me or he really didn't know what it was, but I remember watching him hand the envelope over to Heather without batting an eye. "It's just a scrap piece of paper. Probably just a phone number or something." was exactly what he had said when he did so.

That night I had spent the night in the Geauga County Safety Center, which is the county jail. The next day, I went in front of a very angry looking judge. She was definitely unhappy to see me. After asking me why I had missed, among the other typical questions, she had decided to take pity on me this time. I was let go on another PR bond (that would make the third one that I had been given in a row). Once released, I headed across the street to the local hospital where my mom worked. She then gave me a ride to the county courthouse where I was scheduled to appear for the first custody hearing of many more to come. From there, my mom gave me and Heather a ride back to our apartment (of which we were getting evicted from two weeks later). I of course got the lecture that I had been waiting for since everything went down.

You would think that this would serve as a huge wake-up call. Like one with sirens, blaring horns, and strobe lights. One of those wake-up calls that screamed at you "You're going to kill yourself! You have already lost control and you need as much help as you can get! Drop the crap and grow up!" However, there was no such wake-up call. Instead, I spoke to my wife and had decided that we were going to have "one last Hoorah". That "last one" lasted two weeks and I really didn't think it was ever going to end.

At some point in time, my father-in-law had moved into a rather small house that was just down the road from our apartment. So we grabbed a few items that we wanted with us and walked down to his house. He was also the guy that we usually bought our drugs from, so we figured that was probably be the best option for somewhere to go. I mean, we can't risk running out or, God forbid, becoming sober.

For the next two weeks, Heather and I did nothing but sleep and get high. We were in a seemingly nonstop cycle of dope sickness (withdrawal) and uncontrollable euphoria. For the first time in our relationship, we didn't have any kids to worry about.

We were virtually responsibility free. Therefore, we "lived" like it. We spent all day, every day looking for our next fix. Then we would ride out to anywhere we had to so that we could get it. And finally, we would settle in and get it into our system. This went on for the entire two week period. And that's when I got my wake up call.

My wake up call came in the form of dying. Well, close enough to it at least. We had been looking for our fix all morning, and eventually had gotten ahold of our normal supplier, an individual that I had honestly never met or laid eyes on. We would buy in bulk and attempt to sell some to pay for what we used. At least that was our intentions. In all honesty, I'm about 90% sure that we used way more than we sold. I didn't do the money handling so I'm not all that sure how that went.

Once we got what we were looking for, we got back to where we were staying and ceremoniously (that's the best word that I can use for this) prepared to get as high as we possibly could. I can't remember to save my life in what order we went about shooting ourselves up. I remember all four of us getting the "tools of the trade" out and laying them across the table. I really don't think that I was actually first in the lineup, but it really doesn't matter. I watched as the heroin was mixed with a little water in a spoon. I saw the cotton swab get placed in it and the needle sucking up the mixture. If you're unfamiliar with the process, the cotton was to filter out impurities. A process that I have never fully understood or believed to be effective.

Once it was my turn, I found that I had involuntarily taken my belt off. Actually, this was an automatic reflex once those tools came out. I used it as a tourniquet and cinched it around the bicep of one of my arms (you have no idea how happy I am to announce that I can no longer remember which arm I usually used. I think it was my right, but I really can't remember). Someone else always did the actual injection because I really couldn't. I was absolutely sure that I would've screwed it up. However, I'm positive that if I didn't have anyone around, I would've taught myself pretty quickly. This move helped me prevent any track marks or blowouts in my arm. After the substance was completely in my arm, I loosened my belt to allow the heroin to reach the rest of my body. Every time that I did this, I felt like a little piece of me died. I knew that I was a horrible member of society. I also knew that nobody trusted me or wanted me to be around. I was lower than scum and this stuff was preventing me from caring at all. As long as I was high, I was happy.

I don't remember much from after that. I remember the intense feeling of euphoria washing over my body, and then it went black. I thought that I had just closed my eyes. Almost like I had just blinked and taken just a moment too long to do so. But when I had focused again, quite some time had passed and I was no longer standing in the corner of this tiny kitchen. I was sitting in a chair in the middle of the same kitchen, my head feeling like it weighed four times as much as it actually did. I felt a dull pain from the bridge of my nose (I learned a little later that I had overdosed, collapsed on the floor, and began convulsing. The pain was from where I had smacked my face off of the oven).

I obviously had absolutely no idea what had happened. I remember the first words to come from my mouth. I had murmured "Wait. How did I get here? I could've sworn I was standing." That's when the others had informed me that I had overdosed. I have heard a few different variations of what had happened while I was knocked out, none of which I will be mentioning here because I don't want to give you false information. All I knew at this point was that I survived and everybody must have been so worried. Only one of those is correct.

That's not actually fair because I'm not actually sure

whether or not they were worried and I'm quite sure that they were, at least to some degree. The only one that seemed to show concern was Cathy (Again, the name is changed to protect her identity). She had been very obviously worried. In fact, she had told me that afterwards, she had broken down and balled her eyes out because the reality had set in. As for the rest of them, they were a little different. They actually seemed to be more irritated. No. Wait. That's not the word for it. Agitated? Angry? No. I've got it. They seemed absolutely livid that I had overdosed. For those that don't understand, let me explain why this was how they reacted.

At the time, I really didn't know how to handle that. I was a people-pleaser and I when it came to everybody being angry with me all at once, I had no idea what my next move should be. Therefore, despite the fact that I was walking on shaky legs, I got up, went upstairs, and proceeded to clean. In hindsight, not a great move and that was even pointed out to me by Heather. So after I got thoroughly yelled at, I got up and left. I decided to walk the quarter mile back to my run down apartment, in all of it's trashy glory. I had no idea where to go or what to do. I had never imagined that I would ever experience something like that.

Everybody heard all over the news about addicts that overdose. It was actually a really crazy time for it. You were hearing about it everywhere. I mean there were thousands of overdoses reported every year all of a sudden. But this sickness, this disease, it doesn't let you see any of this and what you do see, you expect it would never happen to you. It whispers in your ear about how that person was just being stupid or reckless. It reassures you that you are in fact smart enough to keep from doing exactly that. And the problem is, this disease is right. Until it does.

# PART 3

# CHAPTER 16

◆ ◆ ◆

I remember trying to pack up our stuff, alone at the apartment. Listening to the eerie silence around me and reflecting on what had just happened. I would stop frequently to either sit and think, or to scrounge around our many hiding places to try to find any amount of any drug that I could. As the residual high faded away, I found myself getting kind of desperate. I found a couple of the cotton swabs that we had already used and began to try to get a "wash" out of them. A wash is when you take the used cotton swabs and try to pull as much heroin out of them as you can. It in itself is a very desperate move, but at this point I didn't care. I wasn't going through withdrawals yet, but I didn't plan on letting myself get even close to it. My plan may have worked, but I found that the "rig" (the syringe or needle) was stopped up with something. I couldn't tell if this was on purpose or not because Heather and I seemed to always be trying to get an edge on the other and sneak more drugs without the other knowing. All I knew was that I was completely up shit creek.

I felt like I was at the end of my rope. In fact, I was still so stuck in my head about where to find my next high and what the hell I was going to do in my situation that I almost missed my phone ringing. And once I saw it, I almost didn't answer. It was my brother who I had recently been informed was in rehab in Cleveland. What could he possibly want? I mean, surely he knows my situation already. That I was about a week away from being forcibly evicted from my only place to live. That I had just lost my kids to the state of Ohio. That I had just been arrested from a warrant from missing a court date. But I figured, what the Hell? Why not answer? After all, he would've been the last person I could think of that would sit there and give me a lecture.

He sounded healthier than any other time I had ever heard him. He almost sounded, dare I say it, happy. The conversation started out typically with the exception of the fact neither of us were asking the other for any kind of favor. I asked how everything was going up there, fully expecting that he would tell me that he was miserable or going out of his mind. Instead, he actually seemed happy to be there. He sounded almost relaxed and at ease. Obviously, when he came back with the same question, my response was a whole lot worse. I proceeded to give him a summary of my last month. The only detail that I had left out was the fact that I had started to use a needle instead of just snorting the stuff. All of our lives we had both been 100% against it, so I was really not trying to upset him or get him to hang up on me. The truth is that nobody else was trying to call and talk to me and it was kind of nice that somebody actually wanted to speak to me.

For about three years or so prior to this moment, my mother would tell me at every chance that I needed to go to rehab. That I needed to get help. I don't know why her approach had never hit home with me, but for some reason I would never listen. I always responded in the same way. "I know mom. I know. Don't worry about me. I've got this." To this day, if I tell my mom that "I've got this," she automatically assumes that I definitely "don't got this." I would roll my eyes and rush away or off of the phone. Not listening to my mother is an issue that I still struggle with today and I am trying to work on it because I already know that she has a lot more life experience than I do. Albeit slowly working on it, but working on it none the less. After all, anybody that has been attending AA meetings for more than one meeting could tell you: "It's progress, not perfection."

My brother took a slightly different approach. I don't know if he did so because he knew what I would respond to or if it was a complete accident that he was able to get through to me more, but he did. Instead of telling me what he thought that I needed to do or lecture me about how bad my life really was, he began to tell me about everything that the Keating Center had to offer and everything that they had done for him and others. I heard all about how well he ate and how he never had to worry about anything besides his own sobriety. He explained how this wasn't your run-of-the-mill rehab with doctors, nurses, and counselors. Instead this place was run by people just like me and him. People who had been addicted to something at one time or another. Therefore, we weren't talking about somewhere that would sit you down and try to talk about your feelings. This was a facility that simply lived by the Big Book of Alcoholics Anonymous.

Because I was a really good and dedicated addict, I had every excuse in the book (plus some that weren't in there) for not going to rehab. I told my brother that I had to work and support my family and he fired back with "Aren't you unemployed?" and "Weren't your kids taken into state custody?" I mentioned how I was a smoker and was nowhere near ready to give up, and he pointed out that the residents there have always helped anybody and everybody with anything, including cigarettes. I made sure to bring up that I was a picky eater, and he followed up with the fact that there is always an abundance of food donated that he already knew for a fact that I would eat. So for the better part of an hour, he and I went back and forth, seemingly without making any ground in either direction. Every excuse that I could make up he had an argument against. It seemed like absolutely no convincing had been done if you were listening to this conversation from outside of it. However, in my head, he was inching me closer and closer by the minute.

The next morning, Heather decided to come back as well. She was angry with me because I hadn't come back by the end of the night, although that part is still a little fuzzy. Therefore, The details may be inaccurate. I clearly remember her being mad at me and I also remember her coming back from her father's house. I remember that while she was mad, she explained that I should've come to her father's to try to get her and that I had failed to do so (She had no idea that I had been there and just never knocked on the door. I decided to give her space instead). The other details are extremely unclear, but you know, drug addict memory and everything.

After coming back, Heather went straight to bed. I tried to lay back down on the couch only to be interrupted by my phone ringing. When I checked it, I found that now my older brother was calling me (my younger brother must've talked to him. I was sure of that). We talked for a very short time and he invited me out to lunch, on him. This struck me as strange because none of my family has ever called me up and invited me anywhere, much less to lunch. However, I really didn't care. Later he swung by and picked me up. I tried to give my wife a quick kiss good bye, but she refused me. So I jumped in my brother's car and we took off for town.

We chose a local bar to have lunch (ironic, right?). And for the record, we never did have lunch. Lunch would imply actually eating something, and to the best of my recollection, neither of us ate a single thing. But then again, eating wasn't exactly the main point of this trip anyhow.

Almost immediately we began to talk about how much I had screwed my own life up in every aspect. And I do mean immediately. Like I kind of remember talking about his family for all of two or three minutes, and then the conversation moved right into the nuclear wasteland that my life had become. I had never seen my brother talk to me with such sincerity. It was absolutely obvious that he was genuinely concerned, and I had never heard him like that, ever. It was both off-putting and kind of nice at the same time. In fact, that's one of the reasons that I had opened up to him so quickly and honestly about my wreckage life.

By the end of our "lunch" (we both had a couple of beers and I don't remember seeing a single bit of food on that table), we had reached the point of the conversation where my brother began to try to convince me to go to rehab. I remember this as being the first time that I had really sat down and taken a look at myself. I looked at everything that I had screwed up and all of the bad choices that I had ever made. And I also found that I had finally recognized exactly what was in front of me. It was the first time that I had seen rehab as more than some kind of lockup. I didn't see it as some kind of punishment or problem that I could be forced into. It was truly an opportunity and I finally saw it as such. An opportunity at a new life and a better future. And for the first time in my adult life, I had made the correct decision. I was finally ready for my first step.

Of course, I fought the notion of simply picking up and going by insisting that I go home for one last night with my wife. Subconsciously, I am absolutely positive that I knew that this was a load of crap. It was right up there with "one last hoorah". However, I really intended to go the next day. I debated with my brother a little while longer about this, but he was able to finally convince me to just go with him, but before I took off with him, I had to make sure that I called Heather. In a way, I was kind of excited about this step that I was about to take. Heather, however, was definitely not.

I called her right outside of the bar after we finished up, and she was not happy at all. I had tried several times to explain to her what was going on and that I had to do this, but she really didn't want to hear it. Actually, she gave me every reason (and excuse) in the book. She brought up everything, especially that the Sheriff's Deputy was there and forcing us out of the apartment, as per the eviction that was granted in court about a month beforehand. Once I finally got her to calm down, she explained that she wanted me to come home just for one more night before I went off to rehab. I had agreed, but was really reluctant to show up until after the Deputy had left. And once she told me there wasn't a Deputy there, it was my turn to get mad, because that would mean that she had lied to me in the beginning of the fight. So I hung up the phone, powered it off, hopped into my brother's vehicle, and took off from Middlefield, ready to take my first step without a single possession on me. From here on out, all I knew I had was me.

Let me back up just a bit and clear something up. The fight on the phone that I had just described is extremely fuzzy. I mean, there are several details that I can't completely remember and what I've just laid out for you to read is all that I actually do remember. However, looking back, maybe she hadn't said the Sheriff's Deputy was there. But what I remember was her saying it. An active drug addict's memory is nothing that should be quoted or cited.

My brother could tell immediately that I was feeling antsy to say the least. I felt like I had the weight of the entire world on my shoulders and mentally I was ready to crack. So he offered a small reprieve. He told me that I could just stay at his house for as long as I felt the need to before I went to rehab. That way, I could stay "off of the grid." From here, only a handful of people were ware of where I was. The only people that knew of my whereabouts were my parents and my brothers (and I think my grandma knew as well now that I think about it) and they were self-sworn to secrecy so that I could just focus on me. I was able to get ahold of some pain killers that I used to help minimize my withdrawal symptoms. This is how I ended my day on September 10th, 2013. From here on out, I was determined to change my story. And for the time being I had to do so hour by hour.

# CHAPTER 17

◆ ◆ ◆

The next day seemed to creep by. My brother and I headed towards the rehab facility some time in the early afternoon. For the entire ride, my stomach was in knots. I was more uneasy and nervous than I had ever been before. I just couldn't shake the feeling that I was essentially placing myself in jail. I really wasn't sure what to expect at all and the only comfort that I had was that my other brother was sitting at the same facility, waiting for me. I tried to plead a case to stay at my older brother's house for a few more nights, but he wasn't hearing any of that. We had stopped by his friend's garage to pick up a shirt that represented the racing team that he was on. Although he couldn't race any longer at the time, he still worked with them all the time, helping with ideas to get the edge on the competition. I still have that shirt somewhere. He had also stopped by a local dollar store to pick up a few essential hygiene products like soap and deodorant. He really made sure to be there for me and when I asked why, he would simply reply "You're an idiot. We're family. What do you mean 'Why'?"

This was the longest hour of my life. I was spending the whole time talking myself out of it. I really didn't know what to expect when I got there. The rehab facility was located in a portion of Cleveland known as the Slavic Village, on Jones rd. Looking around, I saw that everything was run down. It looked like there was a drug dealer on every other street corner. This was where I was supposed to get sober and clean up my act? This was going to be a disaster.

Once we finally got there, I was not any more relieved. My stomach was in my throat. My hands had been more sweaty than any other time that I could remember. My head was pulling me in a million different directions at every thought that had entered it. In short, I was an absolute wreck. The only two things that were keeping me here was the fact that I knew damn well that I needed this help and I was running out of people that were willing to help. That and the fact that I had now gotten myself into a situation where two of my brothers were with me at the same time. If I wanted to make a run for it, I may be able to take on one of them, but definitely not both of them. "God, I'm an idiot." was the only thought that entered my mind at this realization. "You screwed yourself. Good going."

We pulled up to the old brick building that sat between a large white house and a Wendy's, on the east side of Cleveland. A sign with "The Ed Keating Center" was hand painted and hung on the front. Outside of that sign, it was quite obvious that the building had a strong need for work to be done to it. After walking through the front door, I quickly realized the inside was not much different; if so, it was worse. A rather large, bald man stood behind the counter on the right. Sporting a black "Slipknot" shirt, my first impression was that this guy was not messing around and would gladly beat someone up if need be. He was covered in tattoo work and I don't think I saw him smile at all during the first week or so. He handed me a clipboard with some general questions to answer and directed me to the couch that sat nearby. Before I could start with those, my older brother told me that he had to take off to get some things done. He assured me that he would come visit when he could, told me he loved me, and wished me luck. And with that, he walked out the door and an overwhelming feeling of loneliness and abandonment set in.

Upon entering, I was given a clipboard full of different papers that they wanted me to fill out. The normal information was asked for (name, birthdate, history, addiction, etc.) and I filled them out the best that I could. After I finished with these, I handed them over to the "scary guy" and was led deeper into the front office to speak with the man himself. Tommy, the Manager of this facility, was a rather elderly man that sat at a single desk. He had me sit down and explained that nobody was let in without talking to him first. The talk that ensued, however, was one of the most uncomfortable conversations that I had ever had.

I can no longer remember everything that he had said to me verbatim, however, I do remember the gist of it. I also vividly remember how I felt. I was now forced to face exactly who I had become, and that was a horrible experience. He began by asking me why he should give me a bed. He also mentioned that they usually don't accept siblings or others from the same family, at the same time. He continuously reminded me that I had been a terrible person, a horrible son, a failure of a friend, and an overall horrible human being. The more he spoke, the more I sunk into my chair. I couldn't get angry with this stranger because I knew with every ounce of myself that he was telling the truth. This was the first time that I had really looked at who I was and I found that my hatred towards that person was what I had been feeling this entire time. I always thought that I hated myself, but it turns out I just hated this new person that I had turned into.

I had gotten there right after the daily groups had ended. The rest of the day was freed up. I was led to the laundry room where a couple of guys that I had never met in my life were seated. I remember how they were joking around with each other and laughing. How could anybody be in that good of a mood in these conditions? However, I kept remembering my trips to jail and how a lot of those guys simply tried to make the best out of their situation, so I figured that was just what was happening here.

My friend, Head (Of course this isn't his real name, but I don't have his permission to use his real name in here and I think if he read this, he would find it hilarious that I used Head for his name), was quite the stranger to me, but he smiled the entire time and tried to joke around with me as if we knew each other for decades. His partner, Sarge, wasn't quite as smiley as Head was, but he was still very welcoming. He was the one that led me to me room shortly after I had gotten to the laundry room.

I was taken to a very well known room amongst the residents; B3. This was a ten-man room that everybody went to when they first arrived at the east side branch of the Keating Center. Nobody stayed in this room for too long. In fact, I think that I had only wound up staying in this room for about a month at the most. I had been given a top bunk on one of the bunk beds that sat at the end of a rundown (yet surprisingly white) room. Everything about this room was plain. I think the only thing that I could see hanging on the walls was a clock. I quickly stashed all of my stuff (it all fit in one large shopping bag that I had gotten from the dollar store) under the bunk bed, at the end. My brother had bought me a notebook and some writing supplies, so I sat down and started writing. The idea behind it was to keep a journal while I was staying there to record every detail about my stay there. With that being said, I stopped even trying to write at the end of my third day.

I made my way downstairs where the dining room was located and met a couple of the other guys that were staying there. I was expecting to find some kind of staff here as well, but I there never seemed to be anybody around. It was just me and a bunch of other alcoholics and drug addicts. In fact, even the guy that ran the place was an alcoholic that had come to this same facility to get sober at least a decade beforehand. It wasn't until I had gotten myself comfortable and at home until I realized that this entire place was run and operated by alcoholics and drug addicts.

All meals were cooked and prepared by addicts. The night watchmen were addicts. All of the chores to sweep, dust, mop, and taking the trash out was all split up among the residents. All addicts. Even the front office (remember the big scary guy from when I first got there) was run entirely by alcoholics and addicts. This wasn't some "for profit" business model. I came in without even having to prove that my name was in fact Ryan, let alone show proof of insurance. It was amazing and wonderful. A real breath of fresh air to find a place that genuinely wanted to see me succeed and was not drawing a profit off of my problems.

My first day had gone fairly well. I kept to myself most of the time, as I tend to be a pretty shy person (I've been getting a lot better about this). The routine was simple: Wake up and go to morning meditation (this was not as dull or spiritual as it sounds. It was simply a time to share thoughts, concerns, problems, or gratitude and try to reflect on the twelve steps of Alcoholics Anonymous.), eat breakfast, attend two group sessions (others from outside of the facility would stop by to spend time with us and try to help us), then lunch, followed by two more group sessions. After that we had a few hours or so to ourselves to do whatever. Then we would eat dinner and find an AA meeting to go to for the evening (they were already picked out for you for your first two weeks, then you had the freedom to try other meetings around the city). And then after we got back from our various meetings, the rest of the night was, again, ours. At least until count time. This was when we were required to go to our rooms while one of the night watchmen came around to see if everybody had made it back from their meetings and what-not. It was not like jail or prison where you would stand at the end of your bunk, however, you were supposed to go to bed right afterward. Then we would do it all over again the next day.

By the second group that I had gone to on my second day, I was already in my own head. I felt trapped. However, it turned out to get even better. For this group, the moderator that came in insisted that all new guys had to sit in the front row. Larry was a rather intimidating looking individual with a somewhat large build to him. He kept his sunglasses on top of his head and a hoodie did little to hide his size. I spotted him talking to a few of the residents that had been there before me and, from a distance, he seemed like a real nice guy. As we began, however, I learned quickly how he could really be. The reason he wanted all new people in the front row was because was because they WERE the group. He used this as an opportunity every week to remind all of the residents of what they had come from. Actually, I literally just got that. Some of us learn slower than others.

Larry began by talking directly to each of us, working his way from right to left. He would ask us questions and make us say things that none of us wanted to say. Now I know you're reading this and thinking, "Why the hell would I subject myself to this? Why not get up and leave? You're in a free country." It's because I wanted my sobriety that badly and Larry just made you earn it. Plus, we had been actually saying these same things the entire time we were using drugs and alcohol. The words were just never spoken out loud. After your first week, you never actually had to do it again, unless you came back at some point.

He continued to work his way through the front line, one after another. The truth was almost always too much to bare. By using, we were essentially saying that our family, friends, children, loved ones, and selves were of at least lesser importance. The conversations that he was engaging us in made Tommy's from the first day seem like a pep talk. They were absolutely brutal. This was the closest to breaking down that I had ever been. Afterwards I had decided that I had had enough. I had to get out of here.

So I got up and made my way to the front office.

I asked to use a phone at the office (the payphone was not to be used by residents with less than two weeks of time). That day my brother wasn't on site with me, which definitely played into my freaking out. I had to get out of there, and fast. Therefore, my call went straight to my parents. I figured that if there was anybody that I could convince to work with me, it would be them. I couldn't take it anymore and the only other place that I could possibly go was my older brother's house. However, that was definitely not an option because he was the one that had brought me to this place. He was also the one that had talked me into going. So it had to be my parents.

I spoke to my mom in very hushed tones so that the scary guy in the office didn't hear what I was saying. I was positive that if he had, he would cut my call off immediately. Looking back on this experience, I may not have been that far off base, but he would've also just tried to calm me down ("scary guy" happens to be a close and highly-valued friend of mine today).

I gave my mother the same lines. Actually, I gave my mother all of the lines. "I just don't feel safe here." "I need somewhere that I can already just be me." "I promise. I will go to two to three meetings a day in AA. And I'll be sure to get a sponsor." I mean she heard everything from me in this one conversation. If she tried to counter it, I would just switch lanes and hit her with another excuse. For some reason, I couldn't seem to run out of them on that day.

She calmly listened to everything that I had to say (which made me think that it was working. WRONG!) and spoke very little. I wasn't trying to hear anything that she had to say unless the sentence in question started with "Okay." After I had exasperated myself on excuses, finally she spoke. It was only a handful of words brought up the one thing that I hadn't counted on. "I understand Ryan. I do, but I think I have some one here that you need to talk to. Here he is."

I don't know why I was so surprised to hear my brother's voice on the other end of the phone. I really should have put two and two together. He had said the day beforehand that he was going out for an overnight pass. I just didn't figure he would be there being that him and our parents hadn't really ever gotten along after he moved out of the house. What I hadn't taken into account was that my brother's son was living with my parents, so of course he had gone there to spend time with my nephew. Plus, it turns out that they had been really getting along ever since my brother had entered rehab.

"What it do?" he asked me through the phone line (yes, he really talks like that). I then tried all of my excuses on him and wouldn't you know it? None of them worked. "Dude. I'm telling you," he began, "you are exactly where you need to be. Trust me." He went on to explain to me exactly how and why Jones Road would help me. "Have I ever lied to you?" Of course I had to take this opportunity to list off a handful of times that he had in fact lied. "I meant since I went to Jones, Smart Ass." I thought about it really quickly. He really hadn't. "I'll tell you what. Go find my sponsor. If you don't have one yet, try asking him. Explain to him your problems. He has always helped me with mine."

With that we got off of the phones after he assured me that he would be back later that day. I gave the phone back to the scary guy at the counter, Vinny, and sheepishly started to pull away, fully prepared to go disappear into the small crowd of residents. As I handed him the phone, he asked me what the emergency was. Being that I was told that this place was about honesty and I really had nothing to lose, I gave him a brief summary of the conversation that I had. "That's exactly why we don't let new guys use the phone," he said while pointing at the nearby list of rules, "we want you to come in and give it a chance. We want you to know a better life. To realize that you ain't gotta live like that no more." With that, he flashed a quick, friendly smile. It about knocked me over. I didn't know whether I should relax or be frightened. I decided to go with relax.

# CHAPTER 18

◆ ◆ ◆

Behind the rehab/halfway house facility stood a large, separate garage. They had turned it into the only smoking area there was that was indoors. Inside the Smoke Shack you found plenty of places to sit, a radio, some games, and all of the conversation that you could possibly want. On occasion, this area was used to separate a new resident that was going through extreme withdrawal symptoms. That was not the case today though. After I finished talking to Vinny, I made my way to the Smoke Shack, where I found a few of the other. One of the guys was plucking away at a guitar in the corner while a couple of others sat on one of the couches, discussing who-knows-what. I took a seat on one of the chairs and lit one of the cigarettes that my brother had bought for me. Once settled in, I began to lose myself in thought. What should I do now? Should I sneak out and walk to wherever I can get to? Where would I go (being that I was many miles away from the nearest town that I had even known)?

About an hour later, the door to the shack opened up and a strange skinny guy walked in. Slender as can be with a slightly larger nose than he really should've had. He wore a strange looking hoodie while sporting a black beanie. I knew his name was Adam from the day that I had arrived, but that was really all that I knew about him. He squinted slightly while he scanned the room really quick. As soon as he found me he smiled and headed in my direction.

"So what's up Little Ponn?" he asked as he plopped down on the couch that was adjacent to my chair. "What do you think so far?" I explained my issues and we began to talk about them. I couldn't figure out what this guy's angle was, so I finally just asked. "Why do you even care?" I questioned, "I don't even know you." He feigned a hurt look really quickly before returning the smile to his face. "Dude," he started, "You are the older brother of one of my best friends here. I consider your brother to be family. Therefore, if he's my family and you're his family, you are now in fact my family, and there's nothing that you can do about it." This was enough to get a chuckle out of me. Fair enough.

This was the beginning of a small train of people that I had befriended during my first few days. I consider them to be my friends to this day. What I had not known was that my brother had called Adam right after I had gotten off of the phone with him. That first encounter in the Smoke Shack was nowhere near a coincidence. Actually, Adam had coordinated with a few others, and they took turns keeping an eye on me for the first week that I had been there. They are amongst the group of people that I still believe that I owe my life to because they had saved mine.

# CHAPTER 19

◆ ◆ ◆

After I accepted my situation (after all, I had put myself in it), I was able to settle in pretty easily. They have a certain structure to their program there that has helped countless people get back into taking care of their responsibilities. They begin with giving the residents the normal chores (for example clean the bathroom, clean the dining room, clean the front hallway, etc.). These were divided up amongst the residents every week by a designated resident. As you showed responsibility in these chores, Tommy, the guy who ran the place, would choose people to fill special spots that did not rotate. These spots were things like coordinating the chores, working in the kitchen, working in the laundry room, and House Father. The House Father was a position that worked in the front office. Remember Scary Vinny from when I first got to Jones Road? House Father. They enforced the rules and assisted Tommy. They were essentially the care-takers of the house, and due to my behavior once I had settled in, I found myself as one of them.

It was after the last group session of the day and I was sitting back in the smoke shack, relaxing a little bit. I'm aware that this seems ridiculous because it's not like I had just gotten done with work or something. However, in this predicament of mine, there's really not much else that you can do. I was caught by surprise when Vinny came through the doors and scanned the room, only to lock onto me. "Tommy needs to see you" was all that he had to say. My brain automatically started reeling because to me, there was no way this could be good.

I furiously scanned through everything that I knew to try to prepare. What could I have possibly done? Did I witness something that he wanted to question me about? I was only there for a month, so I was pretty surprised that he even knew my name or who I was.

I wound up with no actual idea, which made me even more nervous. "Tommy probably just wants to check up on you and your progress" I silently told myself while I brought myself up to my feet, "I'm sure it's absolutely nothing. In fact, he probably just has the wrong guy." I headed over to the door and joined Vinny. I considered him a friend by now. We got along because I didn't try to bend or break the rules and I made sure to take this thing seriously. After all, we're talking about my life here.

There was a really short walk to be made between the smoke shack and the main brick building, however, this time it felt like it took hours. I'm not sure if Vinny just sensed the uneasiness and nervousness that was coming from me, or maybe he was just too excited to wait. Either way, he stopped me just before we headed into the building. "I have a really important question for you." he said quietly enough that nobody else could hear us, "If you need to, you can take a little while and think about it." All nervousness left me at that very moment. Where was this going? This just got really weird as every ounce of uneasiness that was once being held back by only my skin turned into curiosity and excitement. "Yeah. Okay. Of course. What's going on Vinny?" I watched as the grin slowly creeped across his face, which would have given me the creeps if I hadn't gotten to know him. "Would you want to be a House Father?"

I fully remember my jaw just about hitting the ground. I couldn't believe what I was hearing. Me? A House Father? It was just a month beforehand that I was desperately trying to get out of this place, but now he wanted my help with running the place? This had to be wrong.

"Really? Why me?" I questioned, fully expecting Vinny to tell me that it was a joke. He looked me dead in the eye and told me about how they had just lost the other House Father (apparently he had fallen off of the wagon pretty hard and was spending his days elsewhere, getting drunk. He no longer lived at the facility) and while he was talking to Tommy, he was asked for input on who would make a good replacement. Apparently I was a pretty easy sell. Convinced that this was actually happening, I accepted and started off towards the front office, where I saw Tommy for the second time since I had been here.

Our conversation was much more comfortable and enjoyable than the first encounter. He spoke to me with some actual respect while I sat in awe of this man. I was living at that facility when he had gotten ten years of sobriety under his belt and all you would have to do is watch him to learn how to live sober. He was a shining example of how good the sober life really is and I considered him to be my mentor. And for all intensive purposes from this point on, my boss.

Towards the end of our conversation was when he had finally asked me. For a little while, I had thought that he had brought me to the office for a completely different reason. Maybe he just wanted to check in on me. Or maybe he just enjoyed talking to the residents and just wanted to try to help me more with staying sober. However, neither of those guesses rang true because in the end he had finally asked. "So what do you think Ryan?" he asked after a particularly long-winded lecture, "You want to be one of my House Father?"

"Absolutely! That sounds great to me!" was my response.

Now there was just one issue. What does a House Father do exactly? I mean, I knew that I would be trying to uphold the rules at the house, but that was the extent of my knowledge on the position. After a brief summary, I had a better idea, but I still had to wait until the next day to actually see what was going on.

# CHAPTER 20

◆ ◆ ◆

The next day I woke up and headed towards the office to meet up with Vinny. It turned out that the set up was to have two House Fathers at all times. One should be at the house at all times, so if one of us was going out to the store or something, the other would have to be on site to handle the house. One of the House Fathers (Vinny at that time) was actually on staff. In other words, he was paid to be there. The other (that would be me in this instance) was simply an unpaid resident. This may have been true, but I was still happy to accept the position.

My day was now a little restructured. I would wake up and head down to the office. I would make the coffee for Tommy and take care of anything that needed tended to right there. Usually I would take a little bit of time to start reviewing the meeting sheets (we were to record every meeting we went to, when we went, and have the Secretary of the meeting sign off on our sheets). Then we would head out to the day room to start the morning meditation. After that, while everybody went to do their chores, I would go to the office and clean it up a bit. Usually that was really just running a vacuum over the floor real quickly and dump the trash can. From there, Vinny and I would just stay up in the office, covering the phones and helping with anybody that stopped by. If we got a new guy, I would be the one to take them through their intake paperwork and the other stuff that I had gone through. And if there was any suspicion of any resident using anything, we were the ones to administer the drug test.

The job did come with a fair share of added perks. For example, typically residents aren't allowed to have cell phones. Actually, up until you get two weeks into the house, you're not allowed to use a phone at all (with the exception of having permission from the front office and using theirs). After that, you can use the mounted payphone. I had thought that it would've been a little worse to go without communication for the two weeks, however, the time went by really quickly once I had gotten settled in and comfortable. Once your status turns from half-way to LFW (Looking For Work) you are allowed to have a cell phone again. However, as a House Father, I had to be able to be reached at any time. Whether I was at a meeting, at the store, or just in another area of the house, I had to be reachable. Therefore, I was allowed a cell phone immediately, after only a month in the house.

I had moved out of the 10-man room (B3) and into a 6-man room about two weeks into my stay, which was right across the hall. I was also accruing a surprising amount of things. However, once I became a House Father, it was like the flood gates had opened up. My stay instantly became much easier. For the most part, I wasn't required to go to too many groups anymore. I was also moved into a lockable 4-man room. And being that it locked, I was now able to get certain amenities that I was lacking beforehand. For example, I wasn't allowed to have a TV in my room before. And even if I could, why would I? The doors didn't lock in the other rooms. Therefore, anybody that wound up surrendering to the temptations of addiction could've always walked in and taken anything that I had of any value. But now with a locked room, I no longer had that problem.

I would go out to my older brother's from time to time to visit. When I told him about this new development, he was hellbent on making my stay as comfortable as he possibly could.

He had just replaced a small TV and a DVD player that he had in his garage, so he made sure to give me those, amongst a whole lot more. After he was done giving what he had to me, my bunk easily became the most comfortable out of any of the other 4-man rooms or more. It was fantastic. I had the largest collection of several different scents and such. I also had my personal flat screen TV. Hooked up to that was my own DVD player and a thin PlayStation 2 (which my nephews had generously let me borrow. They had said that they wanted their Uncle Ryan to be as comfortable as possible. They really are amazing kids). In other words, my room had quickly become the place to be.

I had a blast filling in as a House Father. On Sundays, we considered it to be family day. During certain times a resident's family could come out and visit. As my parents hated to be in Cleveland, they would never come out. They would be incredibly supportive, but they would never come out to the actual facility. It's too bad because I bet that my dad would've loved meeting Tommy.

I had a major epiphany around this time during one of the group sessions, albeit a simple one that should have been common sense. We were discussing in terms of alcohol, as an alcoholic had the floor at the moment. He was commenting on feelings of frustration and resentment while drinking. "Why can't I just drink like a normal person?" he had started with. "Why can't I just pick it up casually and then put it back down? These were the thoughts that I constantly had while I was out there drinking." While he continued, I admit that I had let my mind start wandering. I was trying to pay attention, but that question that he had just mentioned was exactly what had gone through my head several times in the past. "Why can't I just use like a normal person? Why do I have to keep going? Why don't I have any control?" That's when it hit me so hard that I had almost literally fallen out of my chair. The rest of the group noticed and I wound up drawing a few stares. I had to share this. And now.

I raised my hand to volunteer this information that had just come to me, knowing how many people were here for the same thing as I was. "You know, that really just hit me." I started, "I have always thought the exact same way. In fact, I was just mulling that over yet again, just now. Why can't I just use like a normal person?" Everybody seemed to be following along with me at this point, all eyes fixated on me and not a single person staring off at a single thing else. "But it just hit me, and it hit me hard." I continued. "That will never be the case. Not because I will never become that person, which honestly, I never will. But this has been bothering me for years and years and it just finally hit me like I ran into a brick wall. Normal people don't use heroin! Normal people don't get addicted to drugs, thus they don't use them. All these years I've been contemplating a question that just makes absolutely no sense!"

I quickly scanned the group, searching for how many people would be breaking into a hysterical laughter. Even a light chuckle or giggle. But there was nothing and for at least half a minute nobody moved. It would seem that nobody else had really thought about this either. From this point on, my sobriety had made a drastic change, and for the better to boot.

My older brother was the only one that would actually stop by, but he usually had a lot going on come Sunday, so I would usually spend those days either watching movies, hanging out in the smoke shack, or meeting the families of the other residents. It was essentially just a day to relax.

# CHAPTER 21

◆ ◆ ◆

Once I got three months in, I was able to advance to the next step in the program, LFW. On one hand, this meant that I could finally get to work and earn money. While being halfway or a House Father, people would come in to give us a hand with finding work. They would call us up when they needed help with something like general labor for an event or to get a nastier job done, ask us if we had however many people that they needed, and we would ask around and try to find someone to fill the spots. Usually, those spots go pretty quickly because it's a house full of halfway residents that can't go out to work and have no money unless family outside of there was supporting you. That was not the case for the vast majority of residents. Those that called in with work would then show up on the time and day that they had planned on and afterward, they would pay us for our services. That way the residents would have a little spending cash for when they went out to meetings. However, being LFW meant that I could find consistent work that I could go to every day, as opposed to just whenever something popped up.

The other side of the coin was that I could no longer be a House Father, as the person that was in that position had to be on site for the vast majority of the day. That job was one that I absolutely loved. It had allowed me to help several people that needed help and I couldn't help but to be reluctant to move on. It was an incredible help to me when it came to my sobriety, not to mention the ways that it helped me with every other aspect of my life. But in the end, I had children that were in foster care and would only be able to be there for a set amount of time. Which meant that I had to go out and start making some kind of money. So I really had to move on.

Throughout my stay on Jones rd, I was given several opportunities to visit with my kids. All of which I took advantage of. My youngest daughter was the only one that didn't seem happy to see me. But then again, she was way too young when she was taken to remember who I really was. She really hadn't been able to form a bond with me at the time. Nevertheless, I took every opportunity that I could get to go see her, and the rest of course.

After about a month of hunting for a job through the internet primarily (I would walk to the library and log on to web sites that had listings for openings) I had finally found one. The individual that I had spoken to had actually made it sound fantastic. When I had shown up on my first day, I was sent out with a woman that was going to help train me and another trainee. Originally I was told that I would be trying to sell some plan for utility bill payments or something like that, but this woman was talking to me about getting people to sign up for cell phone services. We had spent the entire day at the Tower City Mall in downtown Cleveland, talking to whoever would listen to us about signing up for a cell phone (they were essentially "Obama Phones"). That day I had actually enjoyed. I don't know why, but that's when I found out that I'm pretty good at talking to people. Since then, I've used that skill several times for different little projects such as recruiting for the companies that I have worked for.

The very next day, I was encountered by the person who had originally recruited me. He was very friendly and adamant that I move over to his team. That team, I was a lot less comfortable on, the last straw being when I was told that I would be going door-to-door, trying to get people to sign up for some savings plan to save on their utility bills. This was supposed to be done in East Cleveland, which was notorious for being a really bad neighborhood to walk through. Needless to say, I quit within the first hour and a half. This is pretty abnormal for me (my first factory job went for four and a half years and I've been at my current factory job for over five and a half), but there was no way that I was going to push my luck by walking through there.

I may have quit that job on my own volition, but I couldn't help but to feel pretty depressed. After all, it was the only employment that I had managed to find since I had been there. However, it was definitely for the best. It took me a few weeks after that to find any more opportunities, but I had finally found a listing online (craigslist if I'm not mistaken) that was for an opening at a factory. As a guy who has always thrived in an industrial setting, this had definitely seemed like a very appealing opportunity. So I jumped on it immediately. I ran back to the house and called the number from the ad to get the address and make an appointment.

After making a quick visit to our laundry room workers to get some dress clothes from our donation closet, I headed out to buy a bus ticket and begin my adventure to this new opportunity. Up until this point, I really hadn't spent much time around Cleveland, so this was going to take some doing. Luckily I had been collecting the different bus route maps from other residents and the few buses that I had ridden thus far, so I just had to start from my location and work my way back, as each of the maps had also shown where the other bus routes had intersected. Therefore, you really just had to piece your route together from there. It was actually almost fun.

I had arrived at the address the morning of my appointment. To my surprise, I was standing outside of a plain looking office building. I was really expecting to see a factory of some sort, but this would have to do. Upon entering, I looked through the directory and found that this was a temp agency. Suddenly I felt extremely over-dressed and embarrassed to be wearing a three-piece suit. That's okay. I can still do this.

I headed up to the suite that held the Temp Agency and proceeded to apply for the position. And after a short interview and a quick drug screening, I was done and gone. Now it was just a waiting game.

Just after I reached the house, I received the call. They offered me a job at a factory on East 55th. Finally, I could make some kind of money. It was only $8.50 an hour, but money is money and income is income. Finally, it felt like things were looking up.

# CHAPTER 22

◆ ◆ ◆

Shortly after I started collecting my "paychecks" (I've been using direct deposit since this time), I had decided that it was time to take the next step at the house. After LFW, there is one more final step. Three Quarters. You see, you start off being a "Half Way" resident. That was the time that I had the restrictions to go by and chores that had to do with the upkeep of the facility. This is also when I was named as the other House Father. Then you get the opportunity to go LFW. This happened after three months in the house and is when I got the opportunity to look for work. There have also been plenty of residents that had gotten past the LFW step, only to have to regress back to it. I can't stress this enough. That would not be from using or slipping back to old tendencies. This would only be from not being able to meet the requirements of the last step, Three Quarter. To get to Three Quarter, you need to start paying rent. The cost of rent is actually quite low, but if you somehow lose your job for one reason or another, this may be something that you can't do for a while. In that case you would regress. It's as simple as that. You can always go back to Three Quarter at any time you would like, just as long as you can afford the rent.

This last step gives you the most privileges and rights. To over simplify, you can do essentially anything outside of staying out past curfew (which was already more than reasonable) or using drugs or alcohol. That's it. Outside of those stipulations, you are you're own man.

Finally, I had reached the last part of the nine month program. From here it was essentially just maintain. I went to work every day and worked hard. I attended every court date that had been set for me, making sure to dress up in that suit that I had gotten from donation. I went to every visitation that I could set up with my children. And most importantly, I was doing all of this without leaning on drugs or alcohol. With the exception of any minute problems that would pop up, life was for the most part, finally good. Which is probably why all of a sudden, it wasn't.

I had been on the phone with my wife quite a bit after I had gotten a cell phone back. We would either text each other or call and it was rarely a good time. We would argue about everything and I couldn't figure out why for the longest time. For her sake, I'm going to spare everybody from any of the details in this book, but suffice it to say that it was obvious that this marriage was over way before we had thrown in the towel.

The first week after the ring came off of my finger was absolute hell. In fact, I still go to see Tommy from time to time and whenever I am there and someone else approaches us, he never fails to bring up the anguish and the torment that he had watched me going through. I hadn't realized that it was quite so obvious, but apparently, it was. At least it was to Tommy.

I would be found talking to myself and rarely socializing with anybody. I barely ever ate. I slept through the days after I got back from work and didn't get up again until everybody was asleep, at which time I would get up and hang out with my good friend Sleepy (anybody that knows him, will know who I'm talking about), who was the second night watchman at the time. While he rolled cigarettes for the house, we would watch whatever we could find on TV and play card games while I talked to him about my current issues. In many ways, Sleepy helped me out more than most others did and I will always consider him to be an amazing friend.

About a week into this period of time, the hell that I was living increased ten fold. It was when I had found out that she was already seeing somebody else. And to make matters worse, it was somebody that I had considered to be a friend. I had completely come unglued that night while I was on the phone with Heather, and I only became more volatile after he had come to the phone. Apparently, Ben (another fake name) had believed that he could calm me down. Up until that point, he had stayed quiet in the background. I don't know why I even knew that he was there with Heather. She hadn't mentioned it. I just somehow knew. I blew my top completely off and I am surprised that I hadn't awakened anybody, as this was on another night that I had slept all day, and woken up at night.

Let me stop to explain something here. I'm purposely being vague with the details of this night. I'm also keeping the details of my marriage in the later days vague on purpose. Since that time, I have conceded to let bygones be bygones in the interest of the children. I also admit that I had said some really reprehensible things at the time. Today, there is a completely different dynamic. I'm not constantly trying to cut him down anymore and for the most part, we get along. I mean, it's not like we're friends or something. But for the kids, I am more than willing to at least stop cutting him down. Plus, he's not a bad guy to talk to and at least he treats my children with kindness and respect. Either way, for the sake of this book, that is definitely not how I felt at that time.

We continued to fight over the phone for months. It was horrible. Every hour felt like I was being dragged through the flames and embers of Hell itself. I have always been highly critical of myself as well, so I found myself taking it out on myself a lot. However, I definitely made sure to cast plenty of the blame, the overwhelming majority, on the two of them. I had to force myself to focus on anything else at all. All that I could do was take it one day at a time, white-knuckling it the entire time.

The reason for me bringing that part up is quite simple. This is the kind of issue that would make most addicts go back. They would lose themselves in the bottom of the nearest available bottle or shoot to consume record amounts of drugs. But in the end, I had managed to get through unscathed. Now I'm not taking the credit for this. I honestly think that if this happened at almost any other time, I would probably have fallen just like so many others. However, instead I had another resource at my disposal. One that I had never had before. I had the Keating Center.

These guys rallied around me the very second that they had caught a hint of something being wrong. I hadn't even said anything yet. I didn't have to. They just read it on my face like I was a walking suicide note. No. During this time, I never had a single thought of causing any kind of harm to myself. However, I did have to tell them that as well because people seemed worried to even look in my direction. I would pace the floor, time and time again. Slowly wearing a path through the hall and my room. Almost daily I would be fit to be tied without anybody so much as looking at me. With that being said, I made sure not to take it out on anybody else that was there.

I found that what helped me was to help others. I would go out of my way to try and find whatever fresh face that I could. Remembering how it was when I had first gotten there, I would do everything that I could to help them get through it and settle in. I mean, it's a real culture shock to go into the Keating Center. Especially if you have past experience with jails, which is almost always the case in there. What I would do is approach every person that I hadn't seen around there and spoke with them to see if they needed anything. I would ask them about themselves and just do my best to make sure that they felt comfortable. By doing that, in some way, it helped me. My guess is that doing so continuously reminded me of how bad it was out there, how much better life was for me now, and why I didn't want to go back out into that life. Even while I was going through all of the emotional and mental junk that I had with my ex-wife, I would at least work to help out the night watchman and talk through any problems that he was experiencing. But why exactly was this working for me?

It seems to me that once I had taken myself outside of my problems, I was able to breathe a little easier. I was able to focus on something else. Anything else at all. And once that had begun, I was finally able to start pulling myself together.

# CHAPTER 23

◆ ◆ ◆

I continued to live like this for a few more months, and as the weather started to warm up and I approached the end of the nine month commitment that I had signed upon entering the Keating Center, I had realized that I needed to move on. After all, one of my goals was to get my kids back into my life permanently. I had tossed around the idea of staying at the Keating Center for a little bit, but that would mean that I wouldn't be able to have my kids stay with me at all. After all, this was no place for children. I also amused the idea of finding somewhere to live around that area because I already had a job here and I would've loved to stick around near the Keating Center, as I had formed some really strong bonds with some of the other guys that were there. In fact, at that house you can usually find some fantastic sobriety. However, that really wasn't a plausible idea because I was only making minimum wage where I worked. I had figured that I would need at least $10 an hour to be able to get anywhere and, despite the company's level of interest for bringing me on full time, they just couldn't meet me at enough for wages. Therefore, I put in my two weeks notice and on my last day, I made sure to shake everybody's hand and wish them luck, as I've never liked to leave on a bad note from somewhere I've worked. "If you ever," my boss told me, "and I mean ever, need a job. Come back here and I will pick you up in a second." That had effectively left me stunned. This was the first time I had ever heard something other than "Good riddance" or something to that nature. Sobriety was definitely paying off ten-fold already.

I had timed it so that I would have exactly one week between my last day at the factory in Cleveland and the day that I
moved out of the house. I spent that week relaxing with the rest
of the "degenerates" that I had come to call my extended family.
I would either be found laying about my room or hanging around
with some of the guys in the smoke shack. I had sat down with
Tommy about this plan and he told me to keep the rent payment
for the month so that I would have something. He was just a real
class act like that. I even took a trip around Cleveland one of
those days, just for the sake of doing so. I absolutely loved every
one of those guys at the Keating Center I sincerely hope that the
ones that are left were able to keep their sobriety and become
their own personal success stories. If by chance, one of them read
this book or somebody that knows a guy that was in the Jones
Road Keating Center at that time, please tell them to look me up,
if only to let me know that they're alive and kicking.

Moving day finally came and I packed everything that I had
accumulated over the months into my friend's car. After saying a
quick good bye, we were off on the road to my parents' house in
Orwell, Ohio. They really had never been outside of the city very
often, and certainly not since getting sober, so this was kind of an
experience for them. Once we arrived, my children were all waiting for me. The entire point of me going to my parents' house first
was to enjoy a visit with them before reaching my final destin-
ation. We spent the evening having fun and playing with the kids.
I was able to enjoy a fresh, home-cooked meal with my family. It
was perfect and one of the happiest I've ever been.

The following day, my children went back to their foster
home, as they had grown accustomed to, and I continued on my
journey. After some more short good byes, I climbed into the
van with my dad and we hit the road to get to my older brother's

house. As I had been getting closer to finishing up at the Keating Center, I had begun to try to find a place to live. My older brother was the one to offer a place to me. Apparently, he had spoken to his mother about me staying there, and she had no problem with it. This is one of the most beautiful parts about my life, especially since I've become sober. You see, first you should know that I am the oldest child. At least of my mother's children. My older brother is the oldest of my father's children. Therefore, we don't share the same mother, effectively making him actually my half-brother (we don't recognize that though. He is my brother and that's all there is to it). So I hope you can now see why his mother accepting me into their home like she did is so great. When asked, she would simply say, "It's not that Ryan is my ex-husband's kid as much as he is my son's brother." That woman did everything she possibly could for me and I will always hold her in the highest of respects. She is an amazing human being and I will always be there to help her out if I can.

From here, my life has kind of slipped into a monotonous series of events. Within a week I was able to find a job (which is the company that I still work at to this day). After about five or six months, I left and went back to my parents because they had enough room for me to get the kids back. Unfortunately, I had to give the older two up for adoption because I didn't make anywhere near enough to support four children and myself. However, the bright side to that story is that the family that had provided the foster care up until this point, also wasted no time in offering to adopt them. Shortly thereafter, the family picked up and moved to Arizona. I still make an attempt (albeit not a great one) to stay in contact with them. I still believe that was the best thing that I could do for those two wonderful little girls. And if either of them find out about this book, I sincerely hope that they know that I love both of them with all of my heart.

Heather, my now ex-wife, was finally able to clean up her

act. She's since gotten remarried and the two youngest now stay with her. We both work together to take care of them and I am happy to say that I think that she actually kicked the habits.

As for me, it's very hit or miss. There are days that I am on Cloud Nine and everything in the world just feels right. Still, there are also more than plenty of days that I absolutely hate how my life is at the moment. Hate my job and location. Hate every-thing about me. But that's just the thing. That's just life. Every day isn't going to be sunshine and rainbows. But that just makes the days that are that much better. Altogether, I'm very happy with my life. And the days that I'm not, I simply think about one of the more prominent things that Tommy had said to me while I was at the Keating Center. He said:

"Ryan. Keep this in mind. It's always easy to stay sober when everything is working for you. When you've got the house, the job, the girl, the car, and the money. But what about when you don't? What about when the job has to down size and lays you off? When the money dries up because you're unemployed? When you lose the car because you can't pay for it? Or the girl leaves you and takes the house because you don't have a job? What do you have then Ryan? Your sobriety. And be honest, will that be enough for you? Or will you throw that away too? You have to be grateful for everything, including your sobriety be-cause if you take your sobriety for granted, you won't know how to keep it when that's all you have left."

Now, if I find that I'm having trouble with not taking sobri-ety for granted, I just find somebody to help through these same exact issues. In fact, that's what led me to write this book. In fact, if you, the reader, ever need advice or help with an addiction problem, I encourage you to reach out to me. I will respond as soon as I can. I would love to help, just as I was helped to get off of that poison and start turning my life around.

Regardless of what others may argue, I hope you see why addiction is (or at least seems to be) a disease. And I sincerely hope that this book has helped you, in one way or another. If you or someone you know is suffering from addiction, I hope this shows that you can get better. You don't have to live like that any more. If I was able to get sober, anybody can do it. And might I point out, I didn't even need insurance to get into the Keating Center to get help. The only requirement at all is to have the desire to live sober. And if you don't know all that much about addiction or what happens to addicts, I genuinely hope that this has helped you understand what we go through, whether we've put ourselves through it or not. Please remember that my story is of the lighter side of things. My rock bottom could have always been much, much lower than it was, and for many others it is.

# AFTERWORD

I sincerely hope that this book has helped. If you were looking for more insight into what addiction was or maybe just wanted to try "walking in an addict's shoes," I hope this told you all that you needed to know. And if you were looking for help for yourself or someone else, I hope you understand that you really don't have to live like that anymore. There is a better way. Either way, if you have any questions, comments, or concerns, please reach out to me at rponnbooks@gmail.com

Made in the USA
Columbia, SC
29 August 2021